Grade 2

INTERACTIVE Read-Aloud ANTHOLOGY WITH PLAYS

Macmillan/McGraw-Hill

ACKNOWLEDGMENTS

"The First Day of School" from CRICKET NEVER DOES: A COLLECTION OF HAIKU AND TANKA by Myra Cohn Livingston. Copyright © 1997 by Myra Cohn Livingston. Used by permission of Margaret K. McElderry Books, an imprint of Simon & Schuster Children's Publishing Division.

THE ART LESSON by Tomie dePaola. Copyright © 1989 by Tomie dePaola. Used by permission of G. P. Putnam's Sons.

NO DRAGONS FOR TEA: FIRE SAFETY FOR KIDS (AND DRAGONS) by Jean Pendziwol. Copyright © 1999 by Jean Pendziwol. Used by permission of Kids Can Press Ltd.

I WISH I WERE A BUTTERFLY by James Howe. Copyright © 1987 by James Howe. Used by permission of Gulliver Books, Harcourt Brace & Company.

THE AMERICAN WEI by Marion Hess Pomeranc. Copyright © 1998 by Marion Hess Pomeranc. Used by permission of Albert Whitman & Company.

THE STORY OF JOHNNY APPLESEED by Aliki. Copyright © 1963 by Aliki Brandenberg. Used by permission of Simon & Schuster Books for Young Readers, a division of Simon & Schuster, Inc.

Excerpt from A THOUSAND PAILS OF WATER by Ronald Roy. Copyright © 1978 by Ronald Roy. Used by permission of Random House, Inc.

Excerpt from A SPECIAL TRADE by Sally Wittman. Copyright © 1978 by Sally Christensen Wittman. Used by permission of Harper & Row Publishers, Inc.

"The Ugly Duckling" by Hans Christian Andersen, retold by Karen-Amanda Toulon. Copyright © 1989 by Silver, Burdett & Ginn Inc. Used by permission of Silver, Burdett & Ginn Inc.

Excerpt from MAX by Rachel Isadora. Copyright © 1976 by Rachel Isadora. Used by permission of Simon & Schuster Books for Young Readers.

"The Storytelling Stone" a Seneca tale retold by Joseph Bruchac, from KEEPERS OF THE EARTH: NATIVE AMERICAN STORIES AND ENVIRONMENTAL ACTIVITIES FOR CHILDREN. Copyright © 1988, 1989 by Michael J. Caduto and Joseph Bruchac. Used by permission of Fulcrum, Inc.

POLICE PATROL by Katherine K. Winkleman. Copyright © 1996 by Katherine K. Winkleman. Used by permission of Walker and Company.

BURIED IN THE BACKYARD by Gail Herman. Copyright © 2003 by The Kane Press. Used by permission of The Kane Press.

BOY, CAN HE DANCE! by Eileen Spinelli. Copyright © 1993 by Eileen Spinelli. Used by permission of Aladdin Paperbacks, an imprint of Simon & Schuster Children's Publishing Division.

BARNYARD LULLABY by Frank Asch. Copyright © 1998 by Frank Asch. Used by permission of Simon & Schuster Books for Young Readers, an imprint of Simon & Schuster Children's Publishing Division.

Continued on page 230

B

The McGraw·Hill Companies

Macmillan/McGraw-Hill

Published by Macmillan/McGraw-Hill, of McGraw-Hill Education, a division of The McGraw-Hill Companies, Inc., Two Penn Plaza, New York, New York 10121.

Printed in the United States of America

3 4 5 6 7 8 9 10 WDQ 14 13 12 11 10

CONTENTS

Literature Selections

Plays

Think-Aloud Copying Masters

INTERACTIVE Read-Aloud ANTHOLOGY with PLAYS

Developing Listening Comprehension

Read Alouds help to build children's listening comprehension. This anthology offers selections from a variety of genres, including biography, fiction, folktales, nonfiction, and poetry, to share with children. Instruction is provided with each selection to develop specific **comprehension strategies.** Children are asked to **set a purpose for listening,** as well as to **determine the author's purpose** for writing. Using the instruction provided, each Read Aloud becomes an enjoyable, purposeful learning experience.

What Makes a Read Aloud Interactive?

With each selection, **Teacher Think Alouds** are provided to help you model the use of comprehension strategies during reading. Using Think Alouds allows children to listen and to observe how a good reader uses strategies to get meaning from text. After reading, children are given the opportunity to apply the comprehension strategy. Children are asked to "think aloud" as they apply the strategy. By listening to a **student Think Aloud** you can determine if the child is applying the comprehension strategy appropriately and with understanding.

Think-Aloud Copying Masters included in the Read-Aloud Anthology provide sentence starters to help children "think aloud" about a strategy.

Plays and Choral Reading

Reader's Theater for Building Fluency

You can use the plays and choral readings found at the back of this anthology to perform a Reader's Theater with children. Reading fluency is developed by repeated practice in reading text, especially when the reading is done orally. Reader's Theater can help build children's fluency skills because it engages them in a highly motivating activity that provides an opportunity to read—and reread—text orally. As children practice their assigned sections of the "script," they have multiple opportunities to increase their accuracy in word recognition and their rate of reading. Children are also strongly motivated to practice reading with appropriate phrasing and expression.

Performing Reader's Theater

- Assign speaking roles.
- Do not always assign the speaking role with the most text to the most fluent reader. Readers who need practice reading need ample opportunity to read.
- Have children rehearse by reading and rereading their lines over several days. In these rehearsals, allow time for teacher and peer feedback about pace, phrasing, and expression.
- Children do not memorize their lines, but rather read their lines from the script.
- No sets, costumes, or props are necessary.

THE FIRST DAY OF SCHOOL

a haiku by Myra Cohn Livingston

THE ART LESSON

a memoir by Tomie dePaola

Genres: Haiku/Memoir

Comprehension Strategy: Analyze Story Structure

Think-Aloud Copying Master number 6

Before Reading

Genre: Tell children that a haiku is a poem of three lines that do not rhyme. The first line has five syllables, the second line has seven syllables, and the third line has five syllables. Tell children that after the poem, they will hear a type of story called a memoir. A memoir is similar to an autobiography because it is a story about a person's life written by that person.

Expand Vocabulary: Introduce the following words before reading:

artist: a person who creates art

carpenters: people who build wooden structures

lessons: periods of time spent teaching or learning a subject

Set a Purpose for Reading: Have children listen for details that tell about the characters and where the events take place.

During Reading

Read the haiku and memoir aloud. Then use the Think Alouds during the first reading of the memoir. The note about the genre may be used during subsequent readings.

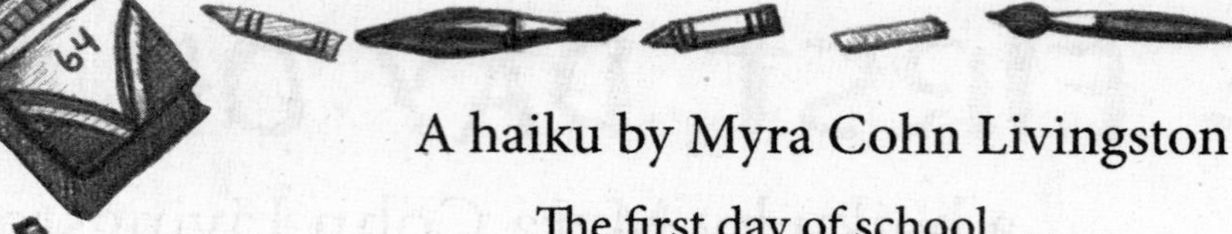

A haiku by Myra Cohn Livingston

The first day of school . . .
does my teacher wonder who
these new faces are?

THE ART LESSON

a memoir by Tomie dePaola

Tommy knew he wanted to be an artist when he grew up. He drew pictures everywhere he went. It was his favorite thing to do.

His friends had favorite things to do, too. Jack collected all kinds of turtles. Herbie made huge cities in his sandbox. Jeannie, Tommy's best friend, could do cartwheels and stand on her head.

But Tommy drew and drew and drew.

His twin cousins, who were already grown up, were in art school learning to be real artists. They told him not to copy and to practice, practice, practice. So, he did.

Tommy put his pictures up on the walls of his half of the bedroom.

His mom put them up all around the house.

His dad took them to the barber shop where he worked.

Tom and Nana, Tommy's Irish grandfather and grandmother, had his pictures in their grocery store.

Nana-Fall-River, his Italian grandmother, put one in a special frame on the table next to the photograph of Aunt Clo in her wedding dress.

Once Tommy took a flashlight and a pencil under the covers and drew pictures on his sheets. But when his mom changed the sheets on Monday and found them, she said, "No more drawing on the sheets, Tommy."[1]

His mom and dad were having a new house built, so Tommy drew pictures of what it would look like when it was finished.

When the walls were up, one of the carpenters gave Tommy a piece of bright blue chalk.

Tommy took the chalk and drew beautiful pictures all over the unfinished walls.

But, when the painters came, his dad said, "That's it, Tommy. No more drawing on the walls."

Genre Study

Memoir: A memoir is similar to an autobiography because it tells about a person's life.

Think Aloud

[1] *I thought this part about Tommy drawing on his sheets was important in this story because it really tells me how much he loved to draw.*

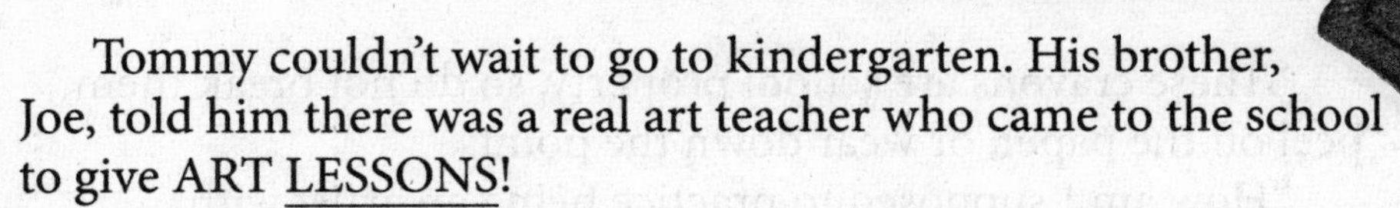

Tommy couldn't wait to go to kindergarten. His brother, Joe, told him there was a real art teacher who came to the school to give ART LESSONS!

"When do we have our art lessons?" Tommy asked the kindergarten teacher.

"Oh, you won't have your art lessons until next year," said Miss Bird. "But, we *are* going to paint pictures tomorrow."

It wasn't much fun.

The paint was awful and the paper got all wrinkly. Miss Bird made the paint by pouring different colored powders into different jars and mixing them with water. The paint didn't stick to the paper very well and it cracked.[2]

If it was windy when Tommy carried his picture home, the paint blew right off the paper.

"At least you get more than one piece of paper in kindergarten," his brother, Joe, said. "When the art teacher comes, you only get one piece."

Tommy knew that the art teacher came to the school every other Wednesday. He could tell she was an artist because she wore a blue smock over her dress and she always carried a big box of thick colored chalks.

Once, Tommy and Jeannie looked at the drawings that were hung up in the hallway. They were done by the first graders.

"Your pictures are much better," Jeannie told Tommy. "Next year when we have real art lessons, you'll be the best one!"

Tommy could hardly wait. He practiced all summer. Then, on his birthday, which was right after school began, his mom and dad gave him a box of sixty-four Crayola crayons. Regular boxes of crayons had red, orange, yellow, green, blue, violet, brown and black. This box had so many other colors: blue-violet, turquoise, red-orange, pink and even gold, silver and copper.

"Class," said Miss Landers, the first-grade teacher, "next month, the art teacher will come to our room, so on Monday instead of Singing, we will practice using our crayons."

On Monday, Tommy brought his sixty-four crayons to school. Miss Landers was not pleased.

"Everyone must use the same crayons," she said. "SCHOOL CRAYONS!"

School crayons had only the same old eight colors.

As Miss Landers passed them out to the class, she said,

Think Aloud

[2] *I can picture in my mind the paint that Miss Bird made, because when I was in kindergarten my teacher made paint the same way. I remember the paint cracking when it dried.*

"These crayons are school property, so do not break them, peel off the paper, or wear down the points."

"How am I supposed to practice being an artist with SCHOOL CRAYONS?" Tommy asked Jack and Herbie.

"That's enough, Tommy," Miss Landers said. "And I want you to take those birthday crayons home with you and leave them there."

And Joe was right. They only got ONE piece of paper.

Finally, the day of the art lesson came. Tommy could hardly sleep that night.

The next morning, he hid the box of sixty-four crayons under his sweater and went off to school. He was ready!

The classroom door opened and in walked the art teacher. Miss Landers said, "Class, this is Mrs. Bowers, the art teacher. Patty, who is our paper monitor this week, will give out one piece of paper to each of you. And remember, don't ruin it because it is the only piece you'll get. Now, pay attention to Mrs. Bowers."

"Class," Mrs. Bowers began, "because Thanksgiving is not too far away, we will learn to draw a Pilgrim man, a Pilgrim woman and a turkey. Watch carefully and copy me."

Copy? COPY? Tommy knew that *real* artists didn't copy. This was terrible. This was supposed to be a real art lesson. He folded his arms and just sat there.[3]

"Now what's the matter?" Miss Landers asked. Tommy looked past her and spoke right to Mrs. Bowers.

"I'm going to be an artist when I grow up and my cousins told me that real artists don't copy. And besides, Miss Landers won't let me use my own sixty-four Crayola crayons."

"Well, well," Mrs. Bowers said. "What are we going to do?" She turned to Miss Landers and they whispered together. Miss Landers nodded.

"Now, Tommy," Mrs. Bowers said. "It wouldn't be fair to let you do something different from the rest of the class.

"But, I have an idea. If you draw the Pilgrim man and woman and the turkey, and if there's any time left, I'll give you *another* piece of paper and you can do your own picture with your own crayons. Can you do that?"

"I'll try," Tommy said, with a big smile.

And he did.

And he did.

And he still does.

Think Aloud

[3] *At first I thought the art teacher would help Tommy be a real artist. But here I find out that she just wants him to copy something. I can see why Tommy is disappointed.*

Retell: Have children draw a picture to show their favorite part of the story. Have them retell the story scene they have illustrated.

Student Think Aloud

Use Copying Master number 6 to prompt children to share what parts of the story were important in showing how much the child liked to draw.

"I thought _____ was important in this story because . . ."

Think and Respond

1. How are the poem and the story alike? Where do they both take place? *Possible response: Both are about school and about learning who new faces are. They take place both at home and at school.* **Analytical**
2. How are the events in the story organized? *Possible response: The author tells about when Tommy was young and then mentions that he goes to kindergarten, then first grade.* **Genre**
3. What is the author's purpose for writing this story and how does it relate to you? *Possible responses: to tell the story about why and how he (the author) became an artist; it makes me think about what I want to be when I grow up.* **Author's Purpose**

The Lion and the Mouse

an Aesop's fable

retold by Margaret H. Lippert

Genre: Fable

Comprehension Strategy: Analyze Story Structure

Think-Aloud Copying Master number 1

Before Reading

Genre: Tell children that a fable is a short story that has a moral. A moral is a lesson taught by the fable. Many fables have been told and retold for thousands of years.

Expand Vocabulary: The following words should be introduced before reading:

lair: a lion's den or home

struggled: made a great physical effort

gnawed: chewed

Set a Purpose for Reading: Have children listen to find out what the moral or lesson of the story is.

During Reading

Use the Think Alouds during the first reading of the story. Notes about the genre may be used during subsequent readings.

The Lion and the Mouse

an Aesop's fable
retold by Margaret H. Lippert

Once, long ago, a lion lay asleep in his lair. A tiny mouse looking for food entered the cave and scurried across the floor. Because it was dark in the cave, he couldn't see the lion in his way. The mouse ran over the lion's foot, and the lion woke up.

The frightened mouse tried to escape, but the lion moved swiftly. He caught the mouse with his paw, and lifted the mouse toward his open jaws. "You will be a tender morsel," roared the lion.

"Don't eat me," pleaded the mouse. "If you let me go I will repay your kindness some day."[1]

"YOU?" roared the lion. "How could a little creature like you help a mighty beast like me?"

"Let me go, and you will see," replied the mouse. The lion was amused by the idea that the little mouse could help him, so he let the mouse go. The mouse ran out of the cave to the safety of his burrow, and the lion went back to sleep.

Many days passed. Then one morning the lion was roaming through the forest. Suddenly he found himself trapped in a net laid by some hunters. He struggled to get free, but as he struggled, the net tightened around him. Soon he could move no more. He lay helplessly in the net.

In terror the lion roared. His desperate roars echoed throughout the forest. The little mouse recognized the voice of the lion who had freed him, and came running to see what was wrong.[2]

When the mouse saw the lion trapped in the net, he knew that he could help the lion. At once the mouse set to work. He gnawed the ropes that bound the lion, and one after another the ropes fell apart. Before long the mouse had made a hole in the net big enough for the lion to squeeze through.

The lion crept out of the hole and turned to the mouse. "You have saved my life," he told the mouse. "I had given up all hope. I thought I would surely die. But you, a tiny mouse, have set me free."

"You see, I was right," responded the mouse. "A little friend can be a big help."

Genre Study

Fable: Most fables have a moral. In this case, the moral is stated at the end of the story.

Think Aloud

[1] *I wonder what the phrase "You will be a tender morsel" means. The mouse says, "Don't eat me!" I think the phrase means that the mouse would be a small treat for the lion.*

Think Aloud

[2] *The animals in this story talk just like real people do. They even have feelings just like people. Right now I think the mouse is worried about the lion.*

Retell the Story: Have children list the important events of the story in the order in which they occurred.

Student Think Aloud

Use Copying Master number 1 to prompt children to share any questions that they have about the beginning, middle, and end of the fable.

Think and Respond

1. Why did the lion let the mouse go? *Possible responses: The lion was amused by the mouse's idea; he wasn't very hungry.* **Inferential**
2. Animals in fables usually act like people. What do the lion and the mouse do that seems human? *Possible responses: They talk; they have feelings; the mouse shows sympathy for the lion.* **Genre**
3. What is the lesson that the author wants readers to learn? *Possible response: Size does not matter. Even little people or things can be useful or helpful.* **Author's Purpose**

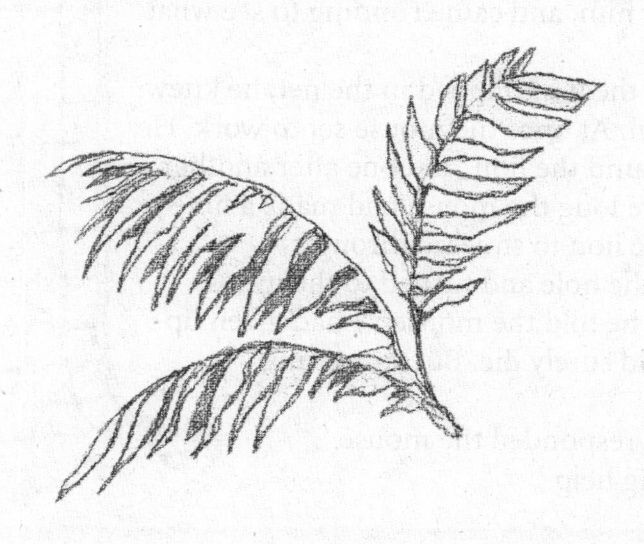

No Dragons for Tea:
Fire Safety for Kids (and Dragons)

a poem
by Jean Pendziwol

Genre: Narrative Poem
Comprehension Strategy: Reread
Think-Aloud Copying Master number 2

Before Reading

Genre: Remind children that a narrative poem is a story with made-up characters and events written in rhyme.

Expand Vocabulary: Introduce the following words before reading:

veered: turned or swerved suddenly
pleaded: begged
wailing: making a long, high-pitched noise
douse: to throw water on something

Set a Purpose for Reading: Have children listen to the poem to find out what the title means.

During Reading

Use the Think Alouds during the first reading of the poem. Notes about the genre and cultural perspective may be used during subsequent readings.

No Dragons for Tea:
Fire Safety for Kids (and Dragons)

retold by Jean Pendziwol

One warm, sunny day at the end of last week,
My mom and I went for a walk to the creek.

As I raced down the hill in my little red wagon,
I veered to the left and smacked into a dragon.[1]

I suppose he could see there was fear in my eyes,
As I jumped to my feet, quite filled with surprise.

He sheepishly grinned and stepped out of the way,
But he seemed so polite that I asked him to play.[2]

He had a cute bear and some other toys, too;
With my shovel and pail, we'd have oodles to do.

We ran to the creek and then on to the bay,
Where we played on the beach for the rest of the day.

Then Mom waved and said, "Now it's time to go eat,
Let's pack the red wagon and head up the street."

It's hard to stop playing with friends old or new,
So I asked if the dragon could come to eat, too.

Mom wrinkled her brow and squinted her eyes,
Looking up at the dragon's incredible size.

I begged and I pleaded, then said, very sweet,
"We won't make a mess; we'll be tidy and neat!"

So at last she said, "Yes. Just this once, I'll agree,
You may have the dragon come over for tea."

We had carrots and apples, thick slices of ham,
With fresh homemade biscuits and strawberry jam,

Cold glasses of milk and a great big dill pickle,
But the pepper we sprinkled sure made my nose tickle!

Think Aloud

[1] *I know that this is made-up because it says that the author smacked into a dragon. I know that dragons are not real.*

Think Aloud

[2] *Dragons can be scary. I wonder why the child is playing with him so comfortably. When I reread, I see it says the dragon was so polite that the child asked him to play.*

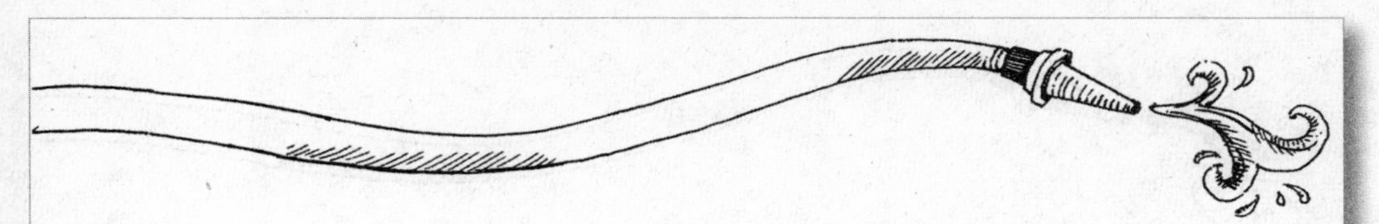

Then the dragon's nose twitched, and he started to wheeze. His eyes misted up, and he blew a great sneeze.

A-A-A-CHOOOOOO!

Well . . . we all know what happens when dragons "a-choo." Flames shot from his mouth and from both nostrils, too.

Our tablecloth sparked and then burst into flame,
And the curtains that hung right beside did the same!

The smoke alarm rang. What a loud, piercing sound!
It meant "Get out fast!" so I dropped to the ground.

The room filled with smoke as I crawled on the floor
And started to make my way to the front door.[3]

The dragon got scared and decided to hide,
But I knew when there's fire, we must get outside.

I grabbed his thick tail and with one mighty tug,
I pulled that big dragon from under the rug.

I crept down the hallway and said, "Follow me,
I know the way out—we must meet by the tree."

So Mom and the dragon and I all met there,
Then that silly dragon went back for his bear!

We ran up and caught him and wouldn't let go,
And I said, "Listen, Dragon, here's what you should know:
Don't ever go back—that just will not do.
We can get a new bear, but we can't replace you."

Since the fire was burning inside of our home,
We went to the neighbor's to borrow the phone.

Mom knew what to dial and said, calm and clear,
"Here's our full street address—send the fire trucks here."

Before very long, down our street they came sailing,
With bright red lights flashing and loud sirens wailing.

[3] *I made a connection when the child started following fire safety rules, such as crawling on the floor. I think I understand the title of the poem now. The author is really talking about fire safety.*

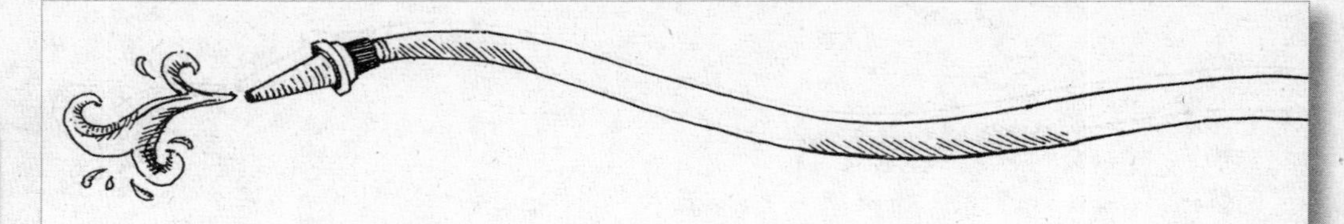

The fire crew rushed to start work on their tasks.
They were dressed in big boots and wore helmets and masks.

They hooked up the hose and ran into the house,
Where they sprayed streams of water in order to douse

The table, the curtains, our lovely snack too,
And it didn't take long till that fire was through.

The fire chief called out the door with a shout,
"The smoke made a mess, but the fire is out!"

My poor friend the dragon knew he was to blame,
So he hung down his head and wept great tears of shame.

One of the fire crew said, "Don't be sad,
You knew what to do, and of that we're quite glad.

"You all got out safely—that's really what matters."
Then she took us to see the big pump truck and ladders.

The dragon put on a shiny red hat,
And I asked to see where the fire crew sat.

She showed us the siren, the hoses and lights,
And the ladders that climb up to reach higher heights.

The rest of the fire crew checked all the rooms,
While a fan in the door blew out gray smoke and fumes.

Then the dragon and I, we sat down for a while.
I reached up and hugged him. He gave me a smile.

The next time the dragon and I want to play,
We'll pack up a picnic and go to the bay.

We are friends, tried and true, the best we can be,
But I'll never again invite dragons for tea!

Genre Study

Narrative Poem: This narrative poem is written in first person. The narrator takes part in the action of the story and uses the words *I* and *me*.

Retell the Story: Have children write a summary of the poem, including some of the fire safety rules.

Student Think Aloud

Use Copying Master number 2 to prompt children to share when they have made a connection about the title of the poem.

Cultural Perspective

Anna, Seventh Duchess of Bedford, reportedly created the idea of afternoon tea in the early 1800s. She came up with the idea of having tea around four or five in the afternoon to fight off the hunger pangs between the midday meal and the end-of-day meal. Afternoon tea is still very much a part of some cultures.

Think and Respond

1. What does the child learn at the end? How did the child learn that lesson? *Possible responses: not to invite dragons for tea; because the dragon set the house on fire* **Critical**
2. Poems can tell about real or make-believe things. What parts of this poem are real? What parts are fantasy? *Possible responses: Dragons are not real. The steps to follow in case of fire are real fire rules, though.* **Genre**
3. What do you think is the author's purpose for writing this poem? *Possible responses: to entertain readers; to teach fire safety rules in a fun way* **Author's Purpose**

a fable
by James Howe

Genre: Fable

Comprehension Strategy: Summarize

Think-Aloud Copying Master number 3

Before Reading

Genre: Remind children that a fable is a short story that teaches a lesson. Point out other fables they have already heard, such as "The Lion and the Mouse."

Expand Vocabulary: Introduce the following words before reading the fable:

defiantly: in a way that shows boldness or disagreement

reflection: a mirror image

envious: wanting what someone else has

gazed: looked at for a long time

Set a Purpose for Reading: Have children listen to find out what lesson is being taught in this fable.

During Reading

Use the Think Alouds during the first reading of the story. Notes about the genre and cultural perspective may be used during subsequent readings.

I Wish I Were a Butterfly

by James Howe

For most of the crickets in Swampswallow Pond, sunrise was a happy time. They came out of their tunnel-dark homes and celebrated the light of day with a fiddler's song.

But the littlest cricket was sad. "I want to stay here," he told his mother. "In the dark?" she asked. "What will you do in the dark? You must come outside to make music."[1]

"Then I won't make music," said the littlest cricket defiantly. "I don't have anything to sing about anyway."

"You don't want to come outside. You don't want to make music. The next thing you know," his mother scolded, "you *won't* want to be a cricket."

The littlest cricket sighed. Had his mother guessed his secret? "I wish I were a butterfly," he said softly. But his mother didn't hear.

"Outside with you this minute," she said.

The littlest cricket knew better than to argue. Out into the bright daylight he went.

But he did not make any music.

The sound of the other crickets fiddling was more than he could bear. "Why are they so happy being crickets?" he asked out loud. "Perhaps they don't know what I do."

"And what is it that you know?" asked a passing glowworm.

The littlest cricket said, "I know that I am ugly. All crickets are ugly."

"Who told you such a thing?" the glowworm asked.

"The frog who lives at the edge of the pond. He told me that I am the ugliest creature he ever saw."

"Well," said the glowworm, inspecting the littlest cricket with care, "you are not the handsomest thing in the world, but you are far from the ugliest. Look at me, I'm no beauty myself."

"But you will change into a lightning bug," the littlest cricket said, "while I will always be a cricket. An ugly, ugly cricket. I wish I were a butterfly."

"There's no use wishing for what can't be," said the glowworm, going on his way. "Being a cricket seems fine enough for me."

Think Aloud

[1] I can picture in my mind what the cricket looks like because I have seen crickets before. I have also heard them making chirping noises by rubbing their legs together. That must be the fiddling and music they're talking about.

"That's easy for him to say," said the littlest cricket. "He will be a lightning bug one day. And the frog who lives at the edge of the pond will never find *him* ugly."

"What do you care what the frog who lives at the edge of the pond has to say?" a ladybug asked from atop a daisy. "If he told me I was ugly, I wouldn't care one bit."

"But who would ever say *you* are ugly?" asked the littlest cricket. "Everyone can see how lovely you are. I am the color of a lump of dirt, but you . . . you are the color of laughter, if such a thing could be."

This amused the ladybug. "Perhaps you are right," she said. "But then you must learn to be content with what you are and not mind what a silly old frog tells you."

"That is easy for *you* to say," said the littlest cricket as the ladybug flew away. "Oh, I wish I were a butterfly."

He jumped onto a lily pad and drifted across the pond. I'll talk to the Old One, he thought. She'll help me.

But seeing his reflection in the water, the littlest cricket started to cry. "Why am I so ugly?" he asked his mirrored self. "Why can't I be—?"

"A dragonfly like me?"

The cricket looked up to see a dragonfly darting about overhead. "I couldn't help but hear your moaning and groaning," said the dragonfly. "It isn't right to be envious of others, you know. It's true that I am a magnificent creature, but so are you in your own way, I am sure."

"Hmph," said the littlest cricket. "You fly around with your whispery wings and your body all covered with jewels and tell me that *I* am magnificent? Please, Mister Dragonfly, go away. You don't understand. You can't understand. I wish I were a butterfly."

"Well you're not a butterfly and never shall be," the dragonfly said firmly. "And wishing is a waste of time."

The littlest cricket blinked, and the dragonfly was gone. It's easy to be happy, he thought, when you are a glistening dragonfly. It's easy to be happy if you are *anything* but an ugly cricket like me.

In the middle of her web on the other side of Swampswallow Pond, the Old One was waiting. "I am good at waiting," she had told the cricket once. "That is a spider's life—spinning and waiting, waiting and spinning."[2]

Think Aloud

[2] *I notice that the author gave the spider the name "The Old One." That tells me that the spider is old and experienced. The spider's name tells me that the spider is wise.*

Today, when the Old One saw the littlest cricket hop off the lily pad, she could see how sad he was. "It's a lovely day," the Old One called out. "And lovely days are too short to wear long faces. What's wrong, my friend?"

"I am ugly," said the littlest cricket.

"Whoever told you that?" asked the spider.

"The frog who lives at the edge of the pond. I am the ugliest thing that ever lived. Oh, how I wish I were a butterfly."

The Old One began to laugh. "Butterflies are pretty enough to look at," she said, "but they are no more special than you."

"Not special?" cried the littlest cricket. "They are the most beautiful creatures in Swampswallow Pond and maybe in all the world. I wish I were as special as that."

The Old One said nothing, but continued to laugh.

"I thought *you* would understand," the cricket said. "You don't envy the butterfly because you're so beautiful yourself."

The spider stopped laughing at once. "You think that I am beautiful?" she asked.

The cricket nodded.

"But I've been told that I'm the ugliest creature in Swampswallow Pond, maybe in all the world."

The cricket looked surprised. "Did the frog who lives at the edge of the pond tell you that?"

"Not only the frog," said the Old One. "Why, if I were to believe what everyone says about me, I would think myself quite, quite ugly. But I don't believe everyone, you see. And I certainly don't believe that grumpy old frog who lives at the edge of the pond. I believe you because you are my friend. You think I'm beautiful, and so I am."

"You *are* beautiful," the littlest cricket said. "But I am as ugly as can be. I still wish I were a butterfly."

The Old One asked the littlest cricket to follow her to the water's edge.

"Look," she said. "What do you see?"

"A beautiful you and an ugly me," replied the cricket. "What do *you* see?"

"Two beautiful friends."

The cricket gazed at himself for a long time. "Am I *really* beautiful?" he asked at last.

"To me you are," the Old One said. "More beautiful than any butterfly I've ever seen."

Genre Study

Fable: Fables usually have animal characters that talk and act as people do.

The littlest cricket looked back at his reflection and, to his surprise, his ugliness began to fade away.

Suddenly, a gust of wind rippled the water.

"Look," said the cricket, turning around. "Your web—the wind has blown away your web."

"Ah, well," the spider said, "then I must begin again. Wait and spin, spin and wait—it's a spider's life. But it would make the time pass more quickly if I had some music to work to."

As the Old One began to spin a new web, the littlest cricket began to fiddle.

And a butterfly, flying past, heard the sound and said, "What beautiful music that creature makes. I wish I were a cricket."[3]

Think Aloud

[3] *This fable is mostly about how a cricket learns to feel good about being himself.*

Retell the Story: Have children act out the story. Assign children to roles as the frog, cricket, mother, glowworm, ladybug, dragonfly, the Old One, and the butterfly.

Student Think Aloud

"I was able to picture in my mind . . ."

Use Copying Master number 3 to prompt children to describe how they picture a favorite part of the story after they have summarized it.

Cultural Perspective

Butterflies symbolize different things in different countries. In Mexico, the butterfly is the symbol of Earth's life and growth. In some countries, butterflies are weather predictors.

Think and Respond

1. Can you relate to the main character in the story? Explain. *Possible response: One time I felt sad and didn't feel like doing anything when someone told me I wasn't good at something.* **Critical**
2. Some fables have repeating events. What is the repeating event in this fable? *Possible response: The cricket meets various animals and has a similar conversation with each.* **Genre**
3. What lesson did the author want to teach in this story? *Possible responses: Don't let negative comments affect you; have confidence in yourself; don't believe everything that other people say.* **Author's Purpose**

The American Wei

a story
by Marion Hess Pomeranc

Genre: Fiction Narrative

Comprehension Strategy: Summarize

Think-Aloud Copying Master number 4

Before Reading

Genre: Remind children that a fiction narrative is a story with made-up characters that retells an event.

Expand Vocabulary: Introduce these words to help students understand the story:

citizen: a person who is born in or becomes a legal member of a country

ceremony: a formal event to celebrate something

loyalty: state of remaining faithful

Set a Purpose for Reading: Have children listen to find out who Wei is and what happens to him in the story.

During Reading

Use the Think Alouds during the first reading of the story. Notes about the genre and cultural perspective may be used during subsequent readings.

The American Wei

by Marion Hess Pomeranc

Wei Fong popped up in front of the hand-carved mirror. The one that had come all the way from China—just as he had.

He touched his hair. He tugged his suit.

"Hurry, we'll be late," he called.

Then he wiggled his tooth. It was very loose. He liked the way it felt as it rocked back and forth in his mouth.

Wei smiled. *Today might be a double-lucky day*, he thought. *In three hours, I'll be an American citizen. And maybe, just maybe, I'll lose my tooth today, too. Then the Tooth Fairy will visit me for the very first time.*

"I'm almost done," said Mama, poking her head out from the kitchen. "We'll have dim sum and hot dogs when we get back.[1] I want everything just right."

"Hurry, Papa," Wei said, running into his parents' bedroom.

". . . Jefferson, Madison, Monroe . . .," Poppa was saying as he straightened his tie.

"Papa, you took your test months ago," Wei said. But he knew his father was proud that he remembered every president's name.

Finally, everyone was ready. The family dashed out the door. They flew down four flights of stairs.

"¡Hasta luego!" called Mrs. Ramos from the landing.

"Good luck today," said Mr. Abramowitz as he walked into the building.

"Mr. Abramowitz, could you take a picture of my family?" Papa asked. "I promised to send Great-Uncle Bing in China pictures of this day."

"Say 'pickled herring,' " said Mr. Abramowitz, snapping the shutter. *Click*, and they were on their way.

"I think it's to the left," said Mama when they arrived downtown. She pointed toward a block filled with tall buildings and whizzing cars.

"I think it's over there," said Papa, pointing the other way.

"I know we'll be late now," said Wei, his tongue rocking the *very* wobbly tooth.

The family ran left. They ran right. They ran all around the block. They found it. The federal courthouse!

"One more picture," said Papa.

Think Aloud

[1] I figured out that even though Wei and his family are Chinese they live like Americans too because they are eating Chinese food (dim sum) and American food (hot dogs).

People hurried into the building. Many were there to become citizens that day, too.

"Where's Wei?" Mama suddenly asked, turning her head.

Mama and Papa dashed back to the street. Papa looked behind a pretzel vendor's cart.

Mama looked under a bench.

"He's dead!" cried mama, running toward the curb.

Wei was down on the ground. His nose was pointed down.

"My son!" cried Papa.

"My tooth!" cried Wei. "I lost it! Don't move!"

Mama and Papa joined Wei on the ground. They ran their hands over the sidewalk. Their fingers followed trails of long cracks.

No tooth.

"We'll have to go," said Papa.

"We'll miss the ceremony," said Mama.

Wei began to cry. "I need my tooth for the Tooth Fairy," he said.

Then Papa jumped up. "I found it!"

Wei's tears got bigger. His sobs got louder. "That's a pebble," he wailed.

"¿Qué pasó?" asked a woman with a cane.

"Our son lost his tooth," Papa explained.

The woman joined in the search.

"Step aside, s'il vous plaît," warned a stout man. He waved *Le Monde*, his newspaper, to direct people around the tooth-seekers.[2]

Soon a family from Poland stopped to help. And a couple from Kenya. And a tall man from Trinidad, too.

"You folks gotta get going!" called a guard near the door. "Things are about to begin."

The search for the tooth sped up.

"Voilà!" said the stout man. "La dent!"

The woman with the cane triumphantly held out something in her hand.

"The tooth!" said the tall man from Trinidad.

"Ząb!" said the family from Poland.

"Jino!" said the couple from Kenya.[3]

Think Aloud

[2] *I notice that the author uses other languages in the story. I think that she does this to show that the other people in the story are from other countries. Maybe some of them are becoming U.S. citizens, too.*

Think Aloud

[3] *This was mostly about how Wei lost his tooth and how lots of people from different countries helped him find it.*

“這顆牙齒!” said Wei’s parents. “Je-kuh-yah-chi!”

Wei wiped his eyes. “My tooth! Thank you,” he said.

The new friends cheered as Mama wrapped Wei’s tooth in a tissue. Then everyone scrambled to the courthouse.

They squished together into an elevator and rode up eight floors. Together, the group slipped through two big doors.

“Step up, don’t be shy,” said a man wearing a badge with a star. He was a federal marshal. “You’ll all be sworn-in citizens soon.”

Mama, Papa, and Wei slid down a long wooden bench.

“I’ve got a lot of people here,” said the marshal to Mama. “Move down, ma’am. There’s always room for one more.”

With a quick wiggle, Mama got closer to the woman from Kenya.

Wei waited patiently as the grownups walked up to a clerk to sign their certificates of naturalization.

“I’ve got something for you,” said Mama when she returned. She gave Wei a large white envelope. Inside was a letter from the President of the United States!

Then the room grew quiet.

“Hear ye, hear ye,” said the clerk. “All rise.”

A woman wearing a long black robe walked in and sat down at the front of the room.

“That’s the judge,” said Papa.

“Be seated,” said the clerk.

“This is a special day. Welcome,” said the judge.

“May I have my tooth?” whispered Wei to Mama.

Wei held his tooth carefully. It was so small! He listened as the judge talked about becoming an American citizen. He saw the marshal open the doors so friends and relatives could watch and listen, too.

Suddenly Mama poked Wei. “Stand up,” she whispered. “It’s time to take the Oath of Allegiance.”

“I hereby declare on oath . . .” the people from many lands said together as they promised loyalty to their new nation.

And when they were done, they were citizens of the United States!

Genre Study

Narrative: Narratives often have time-order words, such as *first, next,* and *finally,* to help readers understand the order in which things happen.

Now the friends and relatives rose, too. They placed their hands over their hearts to join the new Americans in the Pledge of Allegiance. ". . . with liberty and justice for all," the voices rang out.

Then everyone sang "The Star-Spangled Banner."

Some people clapped. Others cried. Wei kissed Papa and Mama. He felt a tear on Mama's cheek.

Wei opened the hand that had been over his heart. He smiled at his tooth.

"One more picture, please," said Papa.

That afternoon, Wei's family and their friends feasted on dim sum and hot dogs. Everything was just right.

When nighttime came, Wei stuck his letter from the president on his wall and slipped into bed. He carefully placed his tooth under his pillow.

"Will the Tooth Fairy know I'm an American citizen now?" he wondered as he fell asleep.

And she did.

Retell the Story: Have children write down the major events that happened to Wei in the correct order. Help children by rereading passages to them.

Student Think Aloud

"I figured out _____ because . . ."

Use Copying Master number 4 to prompt children to share something that they learned or figured out while reading the story.

Cultural Perspective

Many languages are represented in this story. Here is how to say "hello" in those languages:

Spanish—*hola*	French—*allô*	Polish—*witam*
Swahili—*jambo*	Norwegian—*hei*	German—*hallo*

Think and Respond

1. How do you think Wei felt before he went to bed that night? Why? *Possible response: He felt content that he had become a citizen. He might have been anxious that the tooth fairy would come.* **Analytical**
2. Narratives tell events in the order in which they happen. What events made this an important day for Wei? *Possible responses: He lost a tooth in America; he became a U.S. citizen.* **Genre**
3. What do you think was the author's purpose for writing this story? *Possible responses: to introduce readers to other cultures or languages; to show people's common interest in becoming American citizens* **Author's Purpose**

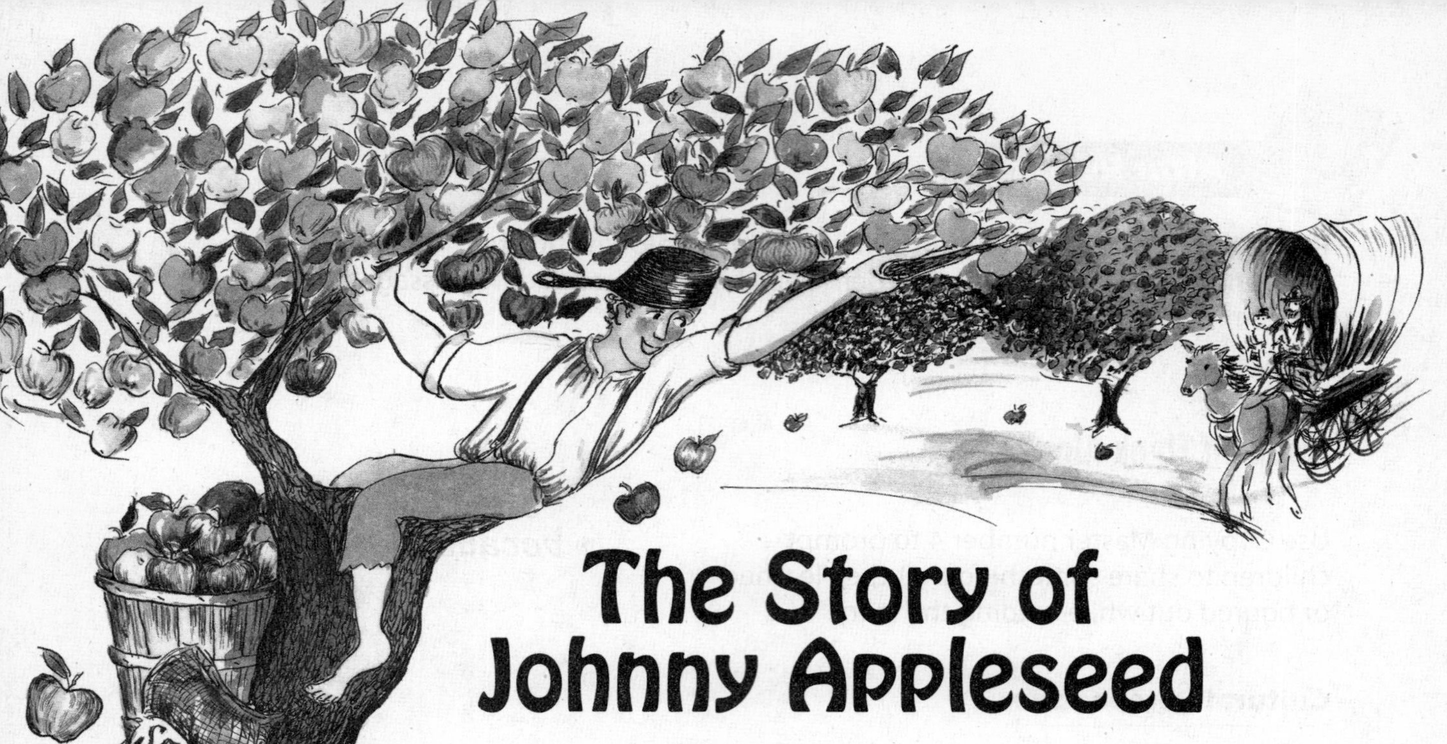

The Story of Johnny Appleseed

a legend
by Aliki

Genre: Legend

Comprehension Strategy: Summarize

Think-Aloud Copying Master number 1

Before Reading

Genre: Explain to children that a legend is a story that has been handed down by people for many years, and that has some basis in fact.

Expand Vocabulary: Introduce the following words or terms to children before reading:

frontier: the land next to an area that has not been settled yet

pioneers: first people to explore a land

settlers: people who come to live in a new place

cider mills: places where apples are made into cider

Set a Purpose for Reading: Have children listen to learn how Johnny Appleseed helped people.

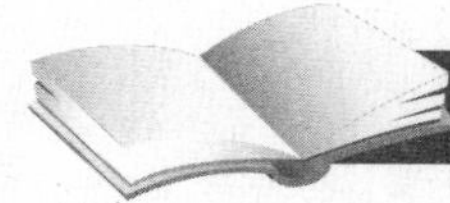

During Reading

Use the Think Alouds during the first reading of the story. Notes about the genre and cultural perspective may be used during subsequent readings.

The Story of Johnny Appleseed

by Aliki

Many years ago when America was a new country, there lived a brave and gentle man named John Chapman. John loved the out-of-doors. He would walk for miles in the woods among the trees and the flowers, happy and alone with his thoughts.

One day, after a long walk, John sat under a tree to rest. He felt the warm sun on his back, and the fresh grass tickling his toes. John took an apple from his sack and ate it. And when he had finished, he looked in his hand at what was left—just a few brown seeds. And John thought: If one gathered seeds, and planted them, our land would soon be filled with apple trees.

John Chapman lived on the frontier, in Massachusetts, where the country had been settled. But every day pioneers were leaving to travel west, where there were no homes or villages and where the only roads were Indian trails.

In their covered wagons, the pioneers made the long and dangerous journey through the wilderness. They wanted to build new lives for themselves in a new part of the country. John Chapman went, too. But he did not travel in a covered wagon. He walked in his bare feet. He carried no weapons, as men did in those days, to protect themselves from wild animals and danger. He carried only a large sack on his back, filled with apple seeds, and his cooking pan on his head.

As he walked, John planted seeds. He gave a small bagful to everyone he saw. Soon, everyone who knew him called him Johnny Appleseed.[1]

Sometimes Johnny stopped for many weeks, helping the pioneers. They cleared the land. They built homes. They planted rows and rows of apple trees. When they were finished, Johnny walked on to help others. But he always came back to see his friends.

Everyone loved Johnny Appleseed, especially the children. When Johnny rested from his planting, the children sat around him, listening to all his adventures.

Genre Study

Legend: Legends often give details about a person who lived long ago. However, these details may not be true but made up to add to the story.

Think Aloud

[1] *The first part of this story tells me that Johnny Appleseed got his name by planting and giving away apple seeds as he traveled.*

Johnny Appleseed walked alone. He slept out of doors, in the woods or by the river. He met wolves and foxes, birds and deer. They were all his friends.

One day, as Johnny was eating lunch, he heard a noise, and three little bear cubs ran from behind a tree. When the mother bear came and saw them playing together, she sat and watched. She knew Johnny Appleseed would not harm her young.

Johnny met many Indians on the way. He was kind to them and gave them seeds and herbs, which they used as medicine. Although the Indians were not friendly to any white men who chased them from their homes, Johnny was their friend.[2]

Johnny did not like people to fight. He tried to make peace between the settlers and the Indians, for he believed that all men should live together as brothers.

On and on Johnny walked, planting as he went. When he needed more seeds, he collected sackfuls from the cider mills. Everyone saved his apple seeds for Johnny. Many years passed. Johnny Appleseed walked on. He visited his friends, and saw with pleasure the many apple trees which covered the land. And he was happy.

But then, one year, there was a long, cold winter. When spring should have come, snow was still on the ground, and frost was on the trees. Johnny could not sleep or eat. He was afraid his trees would die.

As he was walking among the trees one day, Johnny Appleseed fell to the ground. He was very ill. After some hours, an Indian mother and her son passed and saw Johnny lying in the cold. Quickly the boy ran for help. Johnny was carried to their village, not far away.

For many days he lay ill with fever. The Indians gave him medicine and nursed him.[3]

And one day, Johnny Appleseed opened his eyes. He smiled at his Indian friends. He knew they had saved his life. He saw that the sun was warm, and the frost had left the trees. Spring had come at last, and Johnny was well again. But he never forgot his friends and went to see them often.

Think Aloud

[2] I wonder how the Indians knew that Johnny would not chase them from their homes. I think they knew this because Johnny did not carry a weapon and was nice to them.

Think Aloud

[3] I remember that Johnny gave seeds and herbs to the Indians to make medicine. I wonder if this medicine was made from Johnny's gifts. That would be interesting if Johnny's good deeds in the past help save his life.

Retell the Story: Place children in groups of three. Have one group retell the beginning of the story, another the middle, and the last the end.

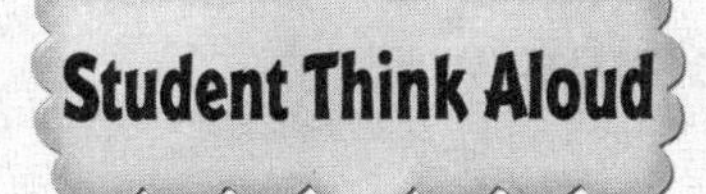

Use Copying Master number 1 to prompt children to share questions they have about the story.

Think and Respond

1. Why do you think everyone loved Johnny Appleseed? *Possible responses: Because he helped everyone; because he gave them apple seeds and told them stories* **Inferential**
2. Legends are written about people who have done great things. Why do you think the author wrote a legend about Johnny Appleseed? *Possible response: He helped many people and was kind to animals.* **Genre**
3. What is the author's purpose for writing this story? *Possible response: to tell readers about Johnny Appleseed* **Author's Purpose**

A THOUSAND PAILS OF WATER

a story

by Ronald Roy

Genre: Fiction Narrative

Comprehension Strategy: Analyze Story Structure

Think-Aloud Copying Master number 6

Before Reading

Genre: Explain to children that a fiction narrative is a story that tells about a make-believe event. Tell children that they will listen to a narrative that tells about one boy's actions.

Expand Vocabulary: Introduce the following words to children before reading:

village: a group of houses and other buildings in a rural area

whale: a large mammal that lives in oceans

tide: the rise and fall of the ocean

villagers: people who live in a village

Set a Purpose for Reading: Ask children to listen to find out who or what needed a thousand pails of water.

During Reading

Use the Think Alouds during the first reading of the story. Notes about the genre and cultural perspective may be used during subsequent readings.

A THOUSAND PAILS OF WATER

by Ronald Roy

Yukio lived in a village where people fished to make their living.

One day Yukio walked down to the sea. As he walked by the edge of the water, he saw a whale. The whale was stuck between some rocks.

Yukio knew that the whale would not live long out of the sea.

"I will help you," he said to the whale. But how? The whale was huge.

Yukio raced to the water's edge. Was the tide coming in or going out?

It was coming in, he decided.

Yukio filled his pail with water and threw it over the head of the huge whale.

"You are so big and my pail is so small," he cried, "but I promise I will carry a thousand pails of water if I must, to save you."

Yukio filled his pail once more. The second pail went on the head as well, and then another and another. Yukio knew he must wet all of the whale or it would die in the sun.[1]

Yukio went to the sea many times. He threw water on the whale's body. Then he threw water on the tail, and then on the head.

Yukio walked to the other side of the huge whale. He was so tired, he sat down. Then he looked at the whale and remembered his promise.

Yukio went back to the sea to fill his pail. How many had he filled? He had lost count, but he knew he must not stop.

Yukio fell, and the very important water ran from his pail. He cried and cried.

Then a wave touched his foot as if to say, "Get up and carry more water. I am coming, but I am very slow."

Yukio filled his pail over and over. His back hurt, and his arms hurt—but still he threw more water on the whale.[2]

Once more he fell, but this time he did not get up.

Genre Study

Narrative: This narrative is written in the third person. A narrator, or an unknown person who is not a part of the story, tells the story.

Think Aloud

[1] *In the beginning of the story, Yukio finds a whale that is stuck. I think he will spend the rest of the story trying to help the whale.*

Think Aloud

[2] *I think the things Yukio does and says are important in this story because they show he is kind to animals and does not give up.*

Yukio could feel himself being lifted.

"You have worked hard, little one," said his grandfather. "Now let us help."

Yukio watched his grandfather throw his first pail of water and go for another.

"Faster!" Yukio wanted to shout, for his grandfather was old and walked slowly.[3]

Then Yukio heard the sound of others. His father and the village people were running toward the sea. They were carrying pails and anything else that would hold water.

Some of the villagers took off their shirts and wet them in the sea. These they placed on the whale's body. Soon the whale was wet all over.

The village people carried water from the sea to the whale many times. Slowly the sea came closer and closer. At last it covered the whale's huge tail. Yukio knew the whale would be saved.

Yukio's father came and sat by him. "Thank you, Father," Yukio said, "for asking the village people to help."

"You are good and you have worked very hard," his father said, "but to save a whale, many hands must carry the water."

Now the huge whale was moving with each new wave. Suddenly a great wave lifted him from the rocks. He was still for just a second, then he swam out to sea.

The villagers watched, as the whale swam farther and farther into the water. Then they turned and walked toward the village.

Yukio, who was asleep, was carried by his father. Yukio had carried a thousand pails of water, and he was tired.

Think Aloud

[3] I see that Yukio's grandfather is helping. I wonder if he really will be able to save the whale. Since he's old and slow, he might not be fast enough to help. Maybe more people will have to help.

After Reading

Retell the Story: Have children retell how Yukio and the villagers saved the whale. Invite them to draw a picture of how the whale was saved.

Student Think Aloud

Use Copying Master number 6 to prompt children to share what they found important in the narrative.

"I thought _____ was important in this story because . . ."

Cultural Perspective

Yukio is a Japanese name that means "gets what he wants." Whales have been an important part of Japanese life for over 4,000 years. Whales were caught for food. The oil and blubber were used for fuel. Ancient Japanese people sang songs in praise of whales.

Think and Respond

1. What kind of person is Yukio? *Possible response: He is determined and caring.* **Inferential**
2. How would this story be different if Yukio was the one telling it? *Possible response: Yukio might tell us more about how he felt.* **Genre**
3. What is the author's message? *Possible responses: People need to work together and help each other. Some tasks are too large for one person.* **Author's Purpose**

A Special Trade

a story

by Sally Wittman

Genre: Fiction Narrative
Comprehension Strategy: Analyze Story Structure
Think-Aloud Copying Master number 2

Before Reading

Genre: Remind children that a fiction narrative is a story that retells a make-believe event. Invite children to recall other narratives they have heard, such as "A Thousand Pails of Water."

Expand Vocabulary: Introduce the following words or terms before reading:

sprinkler: a tool that sprays water on land

walking stick: a cane used to help in walking

railing: a structure used to support walking

harmonica: a musical instrument

Set a Purpose for Reading: Have children listen to find out the meaning of the title.

During Reading

Use the Think Alouds during the first reading of the story. Notes about the genre may be used during subsequent readings.

A Special Trade

by Sally Wittman

Bartholomew is Nelly's neighbor. When Nelly was very small, he would take her for a walk every day in her stroller to Mrs. Pringle's vegetable garden.

Bartholomew never pushed too fast. When they were coming to a bump, Bartholomew always told Nelly.

"Hang on, Nell!" he would always say. "Here's a bump!"

Nelly would shout "BUMP!" as she rode over it.

If they saw a nice dog they'd stop and pet it, but if it was mean Bartholomew would shoo it away.

When Mrs. Pringle's sprinkler was on, he would say, "Get ready, get set, CHAARRRRRRGE!"

Nelly would shout "Wheeeee!" as he pushed her through it. When Nelly began to walk, Bartholomew took her by the hand. "No-No!" she cried, pulling her hand back. Nelly didn't want any help, so Bartholomew offered his hand only when she really needed it. He knew that Nelly was getting older.

Bartholomew was getting older, too. He needed a walking stick now, so they both walked very slowly. When they walked up stairs, they both held on to the railing.

The neighbors called them "ham and eggs" because they were always together. Even on Halloween they were together . . . and on the coldest day of winter when everyone else was inside.[1]

One summer Bartholomew helped Nelly learn how to skate by circling his walking stick. "Easy does it!" he called. Then she skated right over his foot! He wasn't angry, though. He just whistled and held his foot.

The first time Nelly tried to skate by herself, she fell. Bartholomew saw that she felt like crying. He pulled up something from the garden and said, "Don't be saddish, have a radish!"[2] Nelly laughed and ate it. She didn't really like radishes, but she did like Bartholomew.

Before long, Nelly was in school and Bartholomew had become even older. Sometimes Bartholomew needed a helping hand, but he didn't like to take one. So Nelly held out her hand only when Bartholomew really needed it.

Think Aloud

[1] *So far this story tells how Bartholomew helps Nelly in her stroller. I wonder what else he and she will do together. I wonder if he will always help her with things.*

Think Aloud

[2] *I wonder if* saddish *is a real word. I don't think it is, I think the author just wanted to use the word* sad *and make it rhyme with* radish.

Genre Study

Narrative: A narrative often uses dialogue to help readers "hear" characters and understand how they relate with one another.

Think Aloud

[3] *I made a connection when I heard about Nelly pushing the wheelchair over the bump. This reminds me of when Bartholomew pushed Nelly in her stroller at the beginning of the story. Nelly is helping Bartholomew just like he used to help her. It's a good trade between friends.*

Whenever Bartholomew had to stop and rest, Nelly would ask for a story about the "old days." Once after a story, she asked him, "Will we ever run out of things to talk about?"

"If we do," said Bartholomew, "we just won't say anything. Good friends can do that."

Some days they just took it easy and sat on the porch. Bartholomew would play his harmonica, and Nelly would make up the words.

One day Bartholomew went out alone and fell down the stairs. An ambulance came to take him to the hospital, and then he was gone for a long time.

Nelly wrote him every day. She always ended with, "Come back soon, so we can go for walks again."

When Bartholomew came home, he was in a wheelchair. The smile was gone from his eyes.

"I guess our walks are over," he said.

"No they aren't," said Nelly. "I can take *you* for walks now." She knew just how to do it, too. Nice and easy, not too fast.

Just before they came to a bump, Nelly would shout, "Get ready for the bump!"[3] Bartholomew would wave his hat like a cowboy as he rode over it.

If they saw a nice dog they'd stop and pet it, but if it was mean Nelly would shoo it away.

One day when the sprinkler was on, Nelly started to go around it, but she changed her mind.

"All right, Bartholomew. Ready, set, one, two, three. CHAARRRRRRGE!" Nelly pushed him right through it!

"Ah . . . that was fun!" said Bartholomew.

Nelly smiled. "I hope your wheelchair won't rust."

"Fiddlesticks!" he laughed. "Who cares if it does!"

Mrs. Pringle leaned over the fence.

"Seems just like yesterday Bartholomew was pushing you in the stroller," she said.

"That was when I was little," said Nelly. "Now it's my turn to push and Bartholomew's turn to sit . . . kind of like a trade."

Then they sat in the sun to dry. Nelly ate a carrot, and Bartholomew played his harmonica. Nelly could see the old smile was back in Bartholomew's eyes.

Retell the Story: Invite children to retell how Nelly and Bartholomew help each other.

Student Think Aloud

Use Copying Master number 2 to prompt children to share how they made a connection to the story's title.

"I made a connection when . . ."

Think and Respond

1. Why do you think the smile was gone from Bartholomew's eyes when he came home from the hospital? *Possible response: He was sad because he could not walk with Nelly anymore.* **Inferential**
2. How does the use of dialogue help you understand how Nelly and Bartholomew feel about each other? *Possible response: The dialogue shows us that the two have fun with each other and enjoy each other's company.* **Genre**
3. Why do you think the author wrote this story? *Possible response: She wanted to share a story about a special relationship that changed over time.* **Author's Purpose**

The Ugly Duckling

a fairy tale

by Hans Christian Andersen

retold by Karen-Amanda Toulon

Genre: Fairy Tale

Comprehension Strategy: Reread

Think-Aloud Copying Master number 1

Before Reading

Genre: Tell children that a fairy tale is a story that has made-up characters, settings, or events that could not happen in real life. Explain that they will listen to a fairy tale about an ugly duckling.

Expand Vocabulary: Introduce the following words before reading:

beautiful: lovely, pleasing to look at

country: a rural area that has few houses and people

ducklings: young ducks

Set a Purpose for Reading: Have children listen to find out what happens to the ugly duckling.

During Reading

Use the Think Alouds during the first reading of the story. Notes about the genre and cultural perspective may be used during subsequent readings.

The Ugly Duckling

by Hans Christian Andersen
retold by Karen-Amanda Toulon

It was a beautiful day in the country. The sun shone on the green grass, and birds flew in the bright blue sky. The air was full of summer.

There was an old farmhouse not far from a pond. The grass near this pond was soft and tall. It was in this lovely place that a mother duck had made her nest.

It was time for the mother duck to hatch her ducklings. What a long job it was! She had sat on her eggs for days and days. At last, one began to crack and out came a little yellow duckling. The other eggs began to hatch, too, and soon there were many little ducklings.

"Oh, what a big world this is!" said the ducklings. Now they had much more room to move than when they were in the eggs.

"Do you think this is the world?" said their mother. "Why, the world goes way past this nest, right into that garden over there! Now, let me see, are we all here?"

There was still one egg in the nest. "How much longer can this take?" she said. The mother duck sat down on the egg and waited some more. At last she heard a loud CRACK. A big gray duckling came out of the shell. It was very large and very ugly.

The ugly duckling looked at the mother duck and said, "Peep, peep, peep."

"You don't look like one of my ducklings," said the mother. "You are too big and gray."[1] The ugly duckling made a sad peep.

"Well," said the mother, "we will see about you. All ducks can swim. Let us see if you can." With that, the mother duck took all the ducklings down to the pond.

"You must be my duckling," said the proud mother to the ugly duckling. "Why, look how well you swim. Come. Let me show you to my friends," she said and took her ducklings to meet the other ducks.

Think Aloud

[1] *The mother duckling says the big gray duckling doesn't look like her other ducklings. I forget what the other ducklings look like. When I reread I see that they are all little and yellow.*

The other ducks were not at all kind to the ugly duckling. "What a strange duckling!" they said. "Send him away! He is too ugly to be with us."

The ducks picked on the ugly duckling to no end. They bit his neck and legs. As time went on, things did not get any better. The duckling felt so ugly and alone that he ran away.

The sad, little ugly duckling went very far. Night came. He saw a house. The door was open a bit, so he went in.

A woman lived in the house with her cat and her hen. When she saw the ugly duckling, she thought he could lay eggs like a hen.

"Now I will have duck eggs," said the woman. She let the ugly duckling stay.

The cat and the hen were very hard to live with. They picked on the ugly duckling all of the time because he could not lay eggs like a hen or climb like a cat. Once again, the ugly duckling felt sad and alone.

One day the ugly duckling thought of how he missed the country. He thought of the bright sun and the lovely green grass. But more than anything, he wanted to be in the pond. He wanted to swim and feel the water all around him. He told the cat and the hen about it.

"How silly you are, you poor, ugly duckling," they said. "No one who is anything would want to be in water."

"You don't understand," said the ugly duckling.

"Be quiet," said the cat, "and be glad that you have friends who can tell you what is right. Just see to it that you lay some eggs soon." The ugly duckling knew it was time to leave the woman's house, so off he went.

Fall came. The leaves turned red and yellow. Soon they fell off the trees and began to blow about. The wind grew stronger and stronger. The air grew colder and colder.

One day the ugly duckling saw some big birds fly out from behind some trees. He had never seen such beautiful birds. They were white, with long, lovely necks and strong wings.

Genre Study

Fairy Tale: In some fairy tales, the setting could be real but the characters are make-believe.

The ugly duckling watched them fly higher and higher into the air. He felt very strange. He didn't know what the birds were called or where they were going, but he felt so close to them in his heart. He wanted to be with them. As they flew away, the ugly duckling let out a sad cry. He would always remember those beautiful birds.

Winter came. It grew very, very cold. The duckling had to keep moving through the wind and the snow and the ice, so he would not freeze.

It would be too sad to tell all of the hard times the ugly duckling had that winter. Let us just say that the sun began to get warm again, and spring came at last.

One warm spring day, the duckling flew up into the air. His wings felt very strong. He had never gone so high or so fast. He felt proud. Soon he was flying over a lovely garden with a pond. In the pond were those beautiful, white birds he had seen before. When the ugly duckling saw them, he got that same strange feeling again.[2]

"I must be near them," he thought. "I know they will not talk to me because I am so ugly. But I must go to them. They are so beautiful." And then he flew down to the pond.

The ugly duckling swam near the beautiful, white birds. They saw him and swam close to him. The poor duckling put his head down in shame because he thought he looked so ugly. But when he looked down, what did he see in the water? He saw a beautiful, white bird, not an ugly duckling. He was just like the others. He could not believe it was true.

Two children were playing in the garden. They called out with joy, "Look! Look at the new swan. He is the most beautiful swan of all."

Then three great swans came to the new swan and stroked him with their beaks. They, too, thought he was beautiful. He was proud and full of joy, for he had friends at last.[3]

Think Aloud

[2] *It says the Ugly Duckling got that same strange feeling when he saw the big white birds again. I will reread to see what that strange feeling was. When I do, I see that it says he felt close to them in his heart. That is the strange feeling.*

Think Aloud

[3] *I can imagine how the ugly duckling felt when he heard the children call him beautiful. I think he is very happy now that he knows he is a swan.*

Retell the Story: Have children act out the story of the ugly duckling. Assign the parts of the ugly duckling, duck, ducklings, woman, cat, hen, swans, and children.

Student Think Aloud

Use Copying Master number 1 to prompt children to share their questions about the story.

Cultural Perspective

Hans Christian Andersen lived long ago in Denmark. As a child, he was treated much like the ugly duckling in his story. But his many tales became classic children's stories that are told across the world. Encourage children to watch or read another Andersen story and compare it to this one.

Think and Respond

1. How did you feel about the way the animals treated the ugly duckling? *Possible response: I felt sad. I would not want people to treat me that way.* **Analytical**
2. What parts of the fairy tale were make-believe? *Possible response: the animals talking and acting like people and having feelings* **Genre**
3. What was the author's reason for writing the selection? *Possible response: to show readers that they should not treat others poorly just because they may be different* **Author's Purpose**

MAX

a story
by Rachel Isadora

Genre: Realistic Fiction
Comprehension Strategy: Generate Questions
Think-Aloud Copying Master number 3

Before Reading

Genre: Explain to children that realistic fiction is a make-believe story that includes characters and events that could be real.

Expand Vocabulary: Introduce the following words or terms before reading:

barre: a rail attached to a wall, used by ballet dancers

split: a gymnastic action in which the legs are extended in opposite directions

pas de chat: a step in classical ballet

Set a Purpose for Reading: Have children listen to find out what happens to Max when he goes to his sister's dancing school.

During Reading

Use the Think Alouds during the first reading of the story. Notes about the genre and cultural perspective may be used during subsequent readings.

Genre Study

Realistic Fiction: The story is told in the third person point of view. A narrator, who knows how Max feels, tells about Max's day.

MAX

by Rachel Isadora

Max is a great baseball player. He can run fast, jump high, and he hardly ever misses a catch.

Every Saturday he plays baseball with his team in the park. On Saturday mornings he walks with his sister Lisa to her dancing school. The school is on the way to the park.

One Saturday when they reach the dancing school, Max still has lots of time before the game is to start. Lisa asks him if he wants to come inside for a while. Max doesn't really want to, but he says OK.

Soon the class begins. Max gets a chair and sits near the door to watch.

The teacher asks Max to dance with the class, but he must take off his sneakers first.

He stretches at the *barre* (bar).[1]

He tries to do the split.

And then he tries the *pas de chat* (pa-de-sha'). He is having fun.

Just as the class lines up to do leaps, his sister points to the clock. It is time for Max to leave. Max doesn't want to miss the leaps. He waits and takes his turn. Then he must go.

He is late. Everyone is waiting for him.

He goes up to bat. Strike one! He tries again. Strike two! And then . . .

A HOME RUN![2]

Now Max has a new way to warm up for the baseball game on Saturdays. He goes to dancing class with his sister. He leaps all the way to the park.

Think Aloud

[1] *I am able to picture in my mind the dancing school because when I was little I took ballet lessons. There was a barre in my dance class, too.*

Think Aloud

[2] *At first, I thought Max was not going to do well in the game. But then he hit a home run! I guess going to ballet practice helped him.*

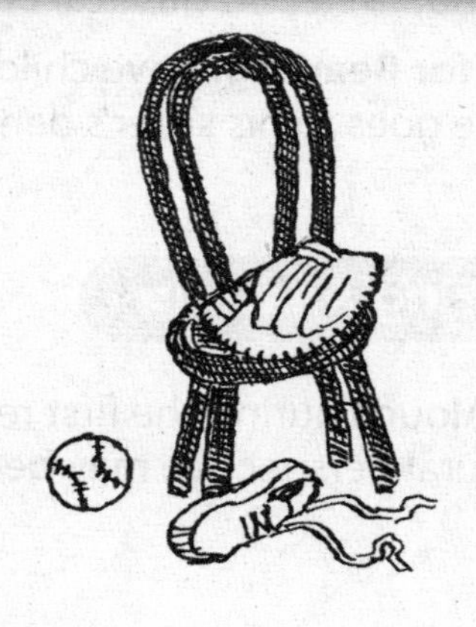

Retell the Story: Invite children to draw a picture of their favorite part of the story. Ask them to explain why it is their favorite part.

Student Think Aloud

Use Copying Master number 3 to prompt children to share any events they could picture in the story.

"I was able to picture in my mind . . ."

Cultural Perspective

Pas de chat is a French word—*pas* means "step," *de* means "of," and *chat* means "cat." It is a jump that is meant to look like a cat's graceful leap.

Think and Respond

1. How do you think Max feels when the teacher asks him to dance? *Possible response: I think he feels nervous because he has never ballet danced before.* **Inferential**
2. Could this have been a true story? How do you know? *Possible response: Yes, Max could have been a real person. All the events are realistic and could have really happened.* **Genre**
3. What do you think was the author's reason for writing this selection? *Possible responses: to show the reader that it is fine for boys to dance and play baseball; to tell a funny story* **Author's Purpose**

The Storytelling Stone

a folktale

retold by Joseph Bruchac

Genre: Folktale

Comprehension Strategy: Generate Questions

Think-Aloud Copying Master number 1

Before Reading

Genre: Tell children that a folktale is a story that has been told many times over many years. In this way, the story is passed down from generation to generation. Remind them of other folktales they might have heard, such as "The Three Little Pigs" or "Goldilocks and the Three Bears." Tell children that the folktale they will hear is from a Native American tribe called the Seneca.

Expand Vocabulary: Introduce the following words before reading:

longhouse: a long and narrow wooden house built by some Native American tribes

partridge: a medium-sized bird

rumbling: making a deep, rolling sound

game: wild animals caught for food

Set a Purpose for Reading: Have children listen to find out what happens when a boy meets a talking stone.

During Reading

Use the Think Alouds during the first reading of the story. Notes about the genre and cultural perspective may be used during subsequent readings.

The Storytelling Stone

retold by Joseph Bruchac

Long ago, there were no stories in the world. Life was not easy for the people, especially during the long winters when the wind blew hard and the snow piled high about the longhouse.

One winter day a boy went hunting. He was a good hunter and managed to shoot several partridge. As he made his way back home through the snow, he grew tired and rested near a great rock which was shaped almost like the head of a person. No sooner had he sat down than he heard a deep voice speak.

"I shall now tell a story," said the voice.

The boy jumped up and looked around. No one was to be seen.

"Who are you?" said the boy.

"I am Great Stone," said the rumbling voice which seemed to come from within the Earth. Then the boy realized it was the big standing rock which spoke. "I shall now tell a story."

"Then tell it," said the boy.

"First you must give me something," said the stone. So the boy took one of the partridge and placed it on the rock.[1]

"Now tell your story, Grandfather," said the boy.

Then the great stone began to speak. It told a wonderful story of how the Earth was created. As the boy listened he did not feel the cold wind and the snow seemed to go away. When the stone had finished the boy stood up.

"Thank you, Grandfather," said the boy. "I shall go now and share this story with my family. I will come back tomorrow."

The boy hurried home to the longhouse. When he got there he told everyone something wonderful had happened. Everyone gathered around the fire and he told them the story he heard from the great stone. The story seemed to drive away the cold and the people were happy as they listened, and they slept peacefully that night, dreaming good dreams. The next day, the boy went back again to the stone and gave it another bird which he had shot.

Genre Study

Folktale: Many folktales are told as if they happened long ago. Often Native American folktales tell how something came to be that made life in the world better or easier.

Think Aloud

[1] *I wonder what the stone will do with the partridge. If the stone was human, it might eat the bird for a meal. But a stone is not human. I think someone might be hiding behind the stone and talking to the boy.*

“I shall now tell a story,” said the big stone and the boy listened.

It went on this way for a long time. Throughout the winter the boy came each day with a present of game. Then Great Stone told him a story of the old times. The boy heard the stories of talking animals and monsters, tales of what things were like when the Earth was new. They were good stories and they taught important lessons. The boy remembered each tale and retold it to the people who gathered at night around the fire to listen. One day, though, when the winter was ending and the spring about to come, the great stone did not speak when the boy placed his gift of wild game.[2]

“Grandfather,” said the boy, “tell me a story.”

Then the great stone spoke for the last time. “I have told you all of my stories,” said Great Stone. “Now the stories are yours to keep for the people. You will pass these stories on to your children and other stories will be added to them as years pass. Where there are stories, there will be more stories. I have spoken. Naho.”[3]

Thus it was that stories came into this world. To this day, they are told by the people of the longhouse during the winter season to warm the people. Whenever a storyteller finishes a tale, the people always give thanks, just as the boy thanked the storytelling stone long ago.

Think Aloud

[2] I wonder why the stone won't speak anymore now that spring is coming. Maybe it thinks the people don't need any more stories since they won't have to stay inside away from the cold.

Think Aloud

[3] At the beginning of the story, I thought someone was hiding behind the stone and telling the stories. But then I found out that it really was a storytelling stone. I can tell this might be a folk-tale because stones do not talk in real life.

After Reading

Retell the Story: Have children draw a picture from the story. Then have them retell the story in their own words, using their pictures as illustrations.

Student Think Aloud

Use Copying Master number 1 to prompt children to share a question they had while listening to the story.

Cultural Perspective

Many Seneca live in what is now New York State. The official language of the Seneca is Ogwehoweh, in which their name translates to *O-non-dowa-gah*, or "great hill people."

Think and Respond

1. How did the stories seem to drive away the cold? *Possible response: The people were so involved in listening to the stories that they didn't think about how cold it was.* **Analytical**
2. Native American folktales often explain how something useful came to be. What does this tale explain? *Possible response: how stories came into the world and how they were passed on over the years* **Genre**
3. What did the author want readers to understand by reading this selection? *Possible response: It is important to tell stories orally and to pass on the tradition of storytelling to each generation.* **Author's Purpose**

Police Patrol

by Katherine K. Winkleman

Genre: Nonfiction/Expository
Comprehension Strategy: Read Ahead
Think-Aloud Copying Master number 1

Before Reading

Genre: Explain that nonfiction selections explain or describe things using facts. All the facts are true and no part of the selection is made up. Tell children that the story they will hear is a nonfiction selection about police officers.

Expand Vocabulary: Before reading, introduce these terms:

safeguard: to protect something or someone from harm

evidence: proof of something

aviation: having to do with aircraft and flying

stakeout: a police surveillance or observation

civilians: ordinary citizens, not in uniform

Set a Purpose for Reading: Have children listen to learn about the different types of police officers and what their jobs involve.

During Reading

Use the Think Alouds during the first reading of the selection. Notes about the genre may be used during subsequent readings.

by Katherine K. Winkleman

Patrol Officers

Both men and women can be police officers. Their job is "to protect and to serve" the public. In most police departments, over half of the staff are patrol officers. Each officer works with a partner to safeguard the community. Police officers patrol on foot and in squad cars, on motorized scooters, and in other vehicles—even on bicycles.

Patrol officers wear uniforms so they can be easily seen by the public.[1]

Detectives

Detectives investigate crimes. The detectives look for clues to answer the questions who, what, when, where, why, and how.

To solve the crime, detectives search the scene, look at physical evidence, and interview witnesses.

Highway Patrol

The highway patrol uses police cars, motorcycles, and even snowmobiles to enforce traffic laws, assist drivers who need help, and catch suspects. Patrol cars have powerful motors and special reinforced tires that prevent skidding during high-speed chases.

Sometimes an aviation unit is called to help the highway patrol catch a suspect.

Aviation

One of the best ways to search is by air. Helicopters are able to hover in one place and fly low to the ground.

They are equipped with special infrared cameras that can find hidden suspects. These cameras detect body heat, which shows up as red against the green background on the monitor.

Harbor and Scuba Units

In areas that have oceans, rivers, or large lakes, the police force includes harbor units and scuba units. Harbor police patrol the waters to make sure that people are boating safely. They also rescue drowning people.

Genre Study

Nonfiction/Expository: The author arranges the facts in this nonfiction/expository piece by listing each type of police officer and describing their jobs.

Think Aloud

[1] *The section on patrol officers is over. But there seem to be many other sections. I didn't know there were that many kinds of patrols. I will read the heads to see what the other sections tell about.*

Mounted Police

Seated upon tall horses are the mounted police. They can be found in the country, in towns, and even in cities. Sitting so high allows the mounted patrol officer to see above the heads of a crowd to spot any trouble.

When an officer and horse are on crowd control duty, a flick of the officer's reins tells the horse whether to back up, swing its hindquarters around, or move sideways, pushing a crowd of people out of the way.

Mounted police are sometimes called "9-foot cops" because if they were measured while riding on a horse, they would be nine feet tall!

Canine Partners

The saying that a dog is a man's best friend applies 100 percent in the canine division, where an officer's partner is a police dog.

Police dogs obey their human partners without question. They are trained to follow the scent trail of suspects, detect illegal food in airports, and perform many other police duties that may be too risky for their human partners.

Undercover Police

Not all police officers wear uniforms. Some are undercover—that is, they're in disguise, so they blend in with the other people around them. Sometimes they look like a friendly neighbor, grandmother, or florist.[2]

Undercover officers often solve cases just by watching, listening, and waiting. They might be undercover for only a day or may be on the same stakeout for months, depending on how important and complicated the investigation is.

Special Forces and SWAT Teams

When people need help, they call the police. When the police need help, they call "special forces." These officers are trained in complicated rescues, and they help in major disasters such as earthquakes and floods. Special forces responsibilities are divided between Special Weapons and Tactics ("SWAT") teams and other highly trained units.

Think Aloud

[2] *I wonder if an undercover officer has ever been in my neighborhood. Undercover agents make themselves look like the people around them, so it would be hard to identify them even if they were right next door to me.*

FBI and State Police

In large disasters or serious criminal situations, the local police are often joined by state police and federal law enforcement agencies, which may include the Federal Bureau of Investigation (FBI) and the Secret Service.

Small Towns

In a small town, there might be one police chief or sheriff and a couple of deputies. Each officer is responsible for patrols, traffic enforcement, and investigation. Everyone in the community knows the officers well, and no one hesitates to ask for their help, even if it is simply to rescue a cat.

Behind the Scenes

Police work depends on cooperation between officers on the front line and the many officers and civilians behind the scenes. Computer technicians, police academy instructors, police dispatchers, telephone operators, secretaries, and many others are essential for catching criminals.[3]

Police dispatchers in big cities might have ten or fifteen emergency calls coming in at once. They need to determine how serious each emergency is, assign police (and send ambulances when needed), and keep speaking with all the different callers.

Think Aloud

[3] I never knew that so many other people were involved in police work. I see the police officers on the streets, but I never see the secretaries, dispatchers, or telephone operators. So I forget that they are involved in helping police officers.

Retell: Have children list one or two facts they learned about police officers while listening to the selection.

Use Copying Master number 1 to prompt children to share any questions they might have about the different kinds of police officers.

Think and Respond

1. Which police unit would help you if you were in a boating accident? *Possible response: the harbor and scuba units* **Analytical**
2. What makes this selection expository? *Possible responses: It describes things using facts. All the facts are true and not made up.* **Genre**
3. What does the author want you to learn about police officers? *Possible response: She wants us to learn about the different types of police officers and what they do.* **Author's Purpose**

BURIED IN THE BACKYARD

a story
by Gail Herman

Genre: Fiction Narrative
Comprehension Strategy: Adjust Reading Rate
Think-Aloud Copying Master number 6

Before Reading

Genre: Explain that a fiction narrative is a story with made-up characters and events. Point out other fiction stories children have heard or read, such as "The American Wei." Tell children that some fiction stories could actually happen, such as the one they are about to hear.

Expand Vocabulary: Introduce the following words:

tape measure: a long roll of fabric, plastic, or paper used for measuring length

exhibit: a display in a museum

guard: a person who protects exhibits in a museum

Set a Purpose for Reading: Have children listen to find out what is buried in the backyard.

During Reading

Use the Think Alouds during the first reading of the story. Notes about the genre may be used during subsequent readings.

Genre Study

Fiction: Fiction has made-up characters and events. This story is made up but could have really happened.

BURIED IN THE BACKYARD

by Gail Herman

"All you want to do is read about dinosaurs!" Katie said.

Ryan smiled. "Dinosaurs are amazing!"

"But it's summer," Katie told him. "We should be outside doing something fun!"

"I'd only go outside if we could swim," Ryan said. "And the town pool is closed."

"Hmmm," Katie said. "What a great idea!"

"What idea?" Ryan asked her.

Katie grinned. "We need a pool!"

Ryan put down his book.

"Mom! Dad!" Katie and Ryan raced into the kitchen. "Can we have a pool in our backyard?"

"A swimming pool?" their mother asked. "That costs too much money."

Their dad laughed. "Way too much. The only way we'd get a pool is if we dug it ourselves." He laughed harder.

Katie pulled Ryan out of the room. "That's it," she whispered. "We'll dig our own pool."

Ryan looked at her like she was crazy. "You know Dad was kidding. Don't you?"

"Sure," Katie said. "But that doesn't mean we can't do it!"

"Where are the shovels?" Ryan asked.

Katie and Ryan went right to work. They dug near the blueberry bushes. Deeper and deeper. It was hard work. But the hole got bigger and bigger.

Thunk! All at once, Katie's shovel struck something hard. "It must be a rock," Ryan said.

Katie dug some more. She peered down the hole. "It's not a rock."

"Maybe it's a log," Ryan said. He started to dig next to Katie. The buried thing was very long and not very wide. Finally they pulled it out of the earth. Ryan brushed it clean.

"It's a bone!" said Katie.[1]

"Wow!" Ryan said. "It's almost as tall as I am. It must belong to a big animal."

"Like a horse," Katie agreed.

Think Aloud

[1] *At first I thought they had just found a rock. I never thought they would actually find a big bone!*

"Or maybe . . ." Ryan caught his breath. "A dinosaur!"

Katie laughed. "A dinosaur bone? In our backyard? You're dreaming.[2]

"Oh, yeah?" Ryan said. He was already heading for the house. "I'm getting a tape measure!" he yelled.

"Four feet! See?" said Ryan. "It could be a dinosaur bone. Let's take it to the museum and look at the dinosaur skeletons!"

"They won't let us in there with a huge bone," Katie said.

"Sure they will," Ryan told her. "Kids bring lots of stuff there. Besides, the lady at the entrance knows me."

"I'll bet she does," said Katie.

Ryan was right. They walked into the museum with no trouble at all.

"I know where the dinosaurs are," Ryan said.

"Big surprise," Katie muttered.

They passed exhibit after exhibit. Ryan was so excited, he didn't look at a thing. He didn't even stop to tie a loose shoelace.

"Oops!" Ryan tripped. The bone nearly fell.

"Great save," Katie said.

Ryan straightened up. He was eye to eye with more bones. He gasped. "Katie! This is what we've got!"

Katie read the sign. "Woolly mammoth." She nudged Ryan. "See? I told you it wasn't a dinosaur!"

"So what!" Ryan said. "This is a prehistoric animal, too! It lived way after the dinosaurs, but still thousands and thousands of years ago."

"Really?" Katie said. "In our backyard!"

"Yep," Ryan said. "Woolly mammoths lived around the same time as the first humans—during the Ice Age."

"The what?" Katie asked.

Ryan waved toward a door. "Follow me."

"The Ice Age was cool," Ryan said.

"You mean COLD," Katie told him.

Ryan grinned. "That, too."

"What if we'd been alive back then?" Katie asked.

"Maybe we would have been mammoth hunters," Ryan said. "And we'd have cooked mammoth meat for dinner."[3]

"Or," said Katie, "maybe we would have had a pet mammoth—or even two!"

"I don't think so," said Ryan.

Think Aloud

[2] *I'm confused. I thought they were digging a swimming pool. Where did the dinosaur bone come from? I must have missed something. I will reread and then try to read more slowly so that I don't miss anything else.*

Think Aloud

[3] *I thought the dialogue was important in this part of the story because it helps explain what Katie and Ryan learn when they go to the museum.*

"Excuse me." A guard stood over Ryan and Katie. "Where did you get that bone?"

"We brought it with us!" Katie said quickly. "We found it in our backyard."

"Well!" The guard grinned. "I think you should meet our scientists!"

That same day Dr. Hook came to Ryan and Katie's house. She talked to their parents about mammoths and the Ice Age and how much she wanted to dig for more bones in their backyard.

Lots of scientists came back a few days later. Shovels flew. Machines dug.

One scientist yelled, "Look at this!" He had found a mammoth tusk.[4] It was very long. Katie and Ryan helped measure it.

"Ten feet! Wow!" Ryan said.

"What did they use their tusks for?" Katie asked.

"To fight with," the scientist said, "and to poke through snow and ice to find grass. Mammoths ate 400 pounds of plants every day!"

"That's a lot of salad!" Ryan said.

Another scientist found a tooth. It was as big as a shoebox!

"Adult mammoths had four teeth at a time," he told the kids. "When a tooth wore out, a new one grew in its place."

Ryan and Katie spent hours and hours at the dig. One day Dr. Hook hurried over to them.

"I have exciting news," she said. "It looks as if there's a whole mammoth skeleton right here in your backyard!"

The next day *everybody* learned about the discovery. Katie and Ryan were on TV! So were their mom and dad.

When the cameras stopped rolling, Mom looked at the kids. "After this, we're going to have a giant hole in the ground," she said. "What do you think we should do with it?"

It wasn't long before Katie was splashing in their brand new pool.

"Come on in," she called to Ryan.

Ryan peered over his book. He gazed at the pool. It was like a giant watering hole. A place where woolly mammoths would have come long, long ago. He could almost see them.

"Ryan!" Katie called. "All you want to do is read about woolly mammoths! Come on in."

Ryan smiled. It *was* kind of hot. So he jumped in, too.

Think Aloud

[4] A woolly mammoth must have looked something like an elephant. The scientist found a tusk, and I know that elephants have tusks. I also know that woolly *means furry or hairy. So a mammoth must have been a giant furry-looking elephant.*

After Reading

Retell the Story: Invite children to act out the story. Assign the parts of Katie, Ryan, Mom, Dad, Dr. Hook, scientists, and a narrator.

Student Think Aloud

Use Copying Master number 6 to prompt children to share something they found important in the story.

"I thought _____ was important in this story because . . ."

Think and Respond

1. Do you think anyone would have found the woolly mammoth bones if Katie and Ryan had not dug in their backyard? *Possible response: No, because the bones had been there so long and no one had found them yet.* **Analytical**

2. What parts of the story could have really happened? *Possible responses: The characters could have all been real. The kids could have found ancient bones in their backyard.* **Genre**

3. The author doesn't directly tell you about the characters, but she includes things in the story that let you know about each person. What does she want you to know about Ryan? *Possible responses: Ryan likes dinosaurs and learning about them. Ryan seems helpful, since he was willing to dig a hole with his sister.* **Author's Purpose**

Boy, Can He Dance!

a story
by Eileen Spinelli

Genre: Fiction Narrative
Comprehension Strategy: Visualize
Think-Aloud Copying Master number 3

Before Reading

Genre: Remind children that a fiction narrative or story can be based on actual events or people, but still contain elements that are made up by the author. Invite children to recall other fiction stories they have heard or read, such as "Buried in the Backyard."

Expand Vocabulary: Introduce these words before reading:

chef: a professional cook
banquet: a formal meal attended by many guests
compliments: words of praise
beamed: smiled broadly, in a proud way

Set a Purpose for Reading: Ask children to listen and try to visualize what Tony looks like and what happens to him.

During Reading

Use the Think Alouds during the first reading of the story. Notes about the genre and cultural perspective may be used during subsequent readings.

Boy, Can He Dance!

by Eileen Spinelli

Many years ago Tony's grandfather had been chef at the City Hotel. He had created graceful ice sculptures. He had designed perfect, pink raspberry molds and white, frosted wedding cakes. He had even learned to cook the mayor's favorite bean soup.

Now Tony's father was chef in the same kitchen of the same hotel. And when it came time for Tony to begin to think about what he wanted to do with his life, his father said: "Think about food."

"Eating?" asked Tony.

"No, cooking," said Tony's father.

This would have made great sense except for one thing. Tony did not want to think about cooking. He wanted to think about dancing.[1]

Even before Tony learned to walk, he was dancing . . . an infant dance . . . kicking his legs and waving his arms so hard that his crib rolled to the other side of the room.

The first day Tony stood up, he started dancing. He danced everywhere. He danced all the time. He danced in the basement and in the attic. He danced at breakfast and in the bathtub. He danced in the backyard and up to the candy store. He even danced on the school bus. That is, until Mr. Wilson, the driver, told him, none too politely, to *sit down!*

"Dancing is fine," Tony's father would say. "I dance myself. With your mother. Once a year. On New Year's Eve." Then, waving his favorite wooden spoon, he would continue, "But I didn't earn my way in the world by dancing. And neither did your grandfather."

And so, early one Saturday morning, Tony's father took Tony to the City Hotel. "If you're going to be a chef when you grow up," he said, "you might as well start learning the business."

Tony's father dumped a pile of lemons on the table. "Maybe you should begin by squeezing lemons for the pies."

Think Aloud

[1] *I can relate to Tony because my parents often want me to do things that I don't want to do.*

Tony did not feel like squeezing lemons. But he didn't want to disappoint his father, either. And so he began.

Squeeze, squeeze, squeeze.

And the squeezing got him to tapping, and the tapping got him to dancing. As he danced he juggled lemons. Tony sailed through the air, juggling lemons . . . right smack into a waiter carrying a tray of empty dishes.

Crash!

The dishes shattered across the floor.

Plop. Plop. Plop.

Three lemons fell right onto the waiter's head.

"Who is that?" growled the waiter.

"That's my son," sighed Tony's father, taking Tony by the hand. "Maybe you'd better chop the carrots for the soup."

Tony stood in front of the big chopping-block table and began.

Chop, chop, chop.

And the chopping got him to tapping, and the tapping got him to dancing. Round and round the table he danced. Right into the woman who brewed the coffee.

"Who is that?" she asked, quite annoyed.

"That's my son," sighed Tony's father. "Tony," he said, "please peel these potatoes, and please stand still!"

Tony's father dumped a mountain of potatoes at Tony's feet. Tony did not feel like peeling potatoes, but he didn't want to disappoint his father, either. So he began.

Scrape, scrape, scrape.

And the scraping got him to tapping, and the tapping got him to dancing. Up one side of the potato mountain and down the other. Right smack into the man who scrubbed pots.

"Who is that?" the man demanded, none too happily.

"That's my son," sighed Tony's father.

He took Tony aside. "This dancing has to stop!"

"The dancing must go on!" cried the hotel manager, Mr. Casey, bursting into the kitchen. He was clearly upset. And whenever Mr. Casey was upset, he'd burst into the kitchen to grumble, complain, and eat cream puffs.

Genre Study

Sound Words: The use of "sound" words such as *chop, chop, chop* helps to show the rhythm that Tony feels as he helps his dad and starts to dance. Authors often use sound words to help readers visualize events.

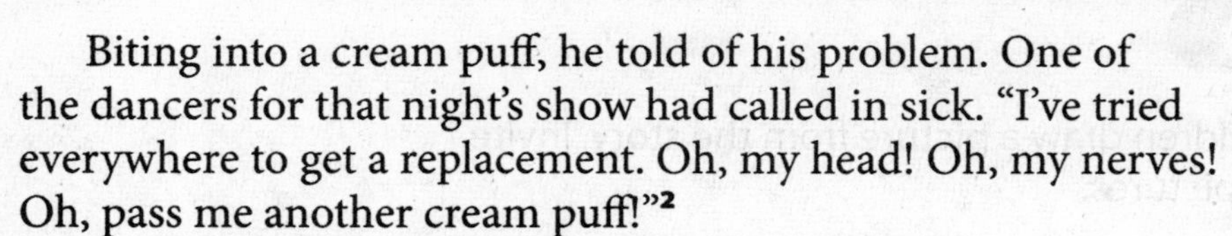

Biting into a cream puff, he told of his problem. One of the dancers for that night's show had called in sick. "I've tried everywhere to get a replacement. Oh, my head! Oh, my nerves! Oh, pass me another cream puff!"[2]

Tony tugged on Mr. Casey's arm. "I can dance."

Mr. Casey stopped stuffing his mouth. "Who is that?"

"That's my son," sighed Tony's father. "I brought him in to learn to cook."

"Does he really dance?"

"Yup," said the waiter.

"He dances!" exclaimed the woman who brewed the coffee.

"Boy, does he dance!" said the man who washed the pots.

With that, Tony jumped up on the table and began dancing. He danced and twirled and kicked and spun until everyone was dizzy.

Mr. Casey looked at Tony's father. "Mind if I borrow your son?"

"Please do!" called the waiter.

For the rest of the day, Tony's father cooked. He seasoned seven hundred french fries. He stirred gallons of carrot soup. He baked nine lovely hams with cherries and pineapples. He made a towering, shimmering salad of cucumbers and lime Jell-O . . . and twenty lemon meringue pies.

That night two hundred people came to the banquet at the City Hotel. They ate everything that was served, and many of them said to the waiter, "My compliments to the chef!" which was music to Tony's father's ears.

But Tony was hearing a different music. All day he had been practicing with the other dancers. Now, with the dinner over, he stood behind the curtain of the City Hotel's grand stage.

The orchestra began to play.

As the curtain went up, Tony began to dance. He *danced* and *twirled* and *kicked* and *spun* around.

Tony's father watched from the open kitchen door.

The man who ran the dishwasher watched, too. "Who is that?" he asked.

"That's my son," beamed Tony's father. . . .[3]

"Boy, can he dance!"

Think Aloud

[2] *I predict the hotel manager will have Tony dance in the show, because Tony loves to dance and was dancing while he was helping with the cooking. Also Tony is there, and the manager needs someone right away.*

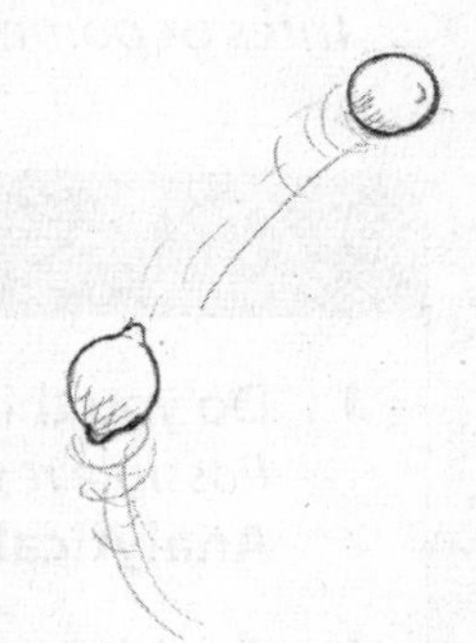

Think Aloud

[3] *I can picture in my mind Tony dancing on the big stage and his father watching from the kitchen door with a big smile on his face. I can tell his father is now very proud of Tony. The author says he "beamed."*

After Reading

Retell the Story: Have children draw a picture from the story. Invite children to describe their pictures.

Student Think Aloud

"I was able to picture in my mind . . ."

Use Copying Master number 3 to prompt children to share something that they could visualize while listening to the story.

Cultural Perspective

In the United States, fried potato sticks are called *french fries.* They are known as *chips* in Great Britain and Ireland, and *frites* or *pommes frites* in Belgium, France, and Germany.

Think and Respond

1. Do you think Tony's father will still want him to be a chef? Why or why not? *Possible response: No, because he found out that his son could really be a dancer.* **Analytical**

2. Could this selection have happened in real life? Why is this story considered to be fiction? *Possible response: The story could have really happened, but it is fiction because the author made up the characters and story and probably exaggerated some of the actions.* **Genre**

3. What is the author's message in this story? *Possible responses: to show the reader that people can have jobs doing what they enjoy; to show that people don't always have to be what their parents want them to be* **Author's Purpose**

Barnyard Lullaby

a story

by Frank Asch

Genre: Fiction Narrative

Comprehension Strategy: Generate Questions

Think-Aloud Copying Master number 1

Before Reading

Genre: Tell children that a narrative is a story told in the order in which events happen. Help children recall other narratives they have read or heard.

Expand Vocabulary: Introduce the following words before reading:

lullaby: a gentle song for soothing a child to sleep

drift: to move gently along

wallowing: rolling around in something

grazed: ate grass in a field

Set a Purpose for Reading: Ask children to listen to picture in their minds what the animals do one night on a farm.

During Reading

Use the Think Alouds during the first reading of the story. Notes about the genre may be used during subsequent readings.

Genre Study

Narrative: The use of lullabies makes the selection more interesting for readers and connects each part of the narrative together.

Barnyard Lullaby

by Frank Asch

One night, when the barnyard was quiet, Mother Hen began to sing. To the farmer in his bed her song sounded like so much cluck, cluck, clucking.

But her chicks heard the music and understood the words. To them it was a beautiful lullaby that went like this:

> Gather round, my children,
> Cuddle as I sing,
> Let yourselves grow sleepy,
> Safe beneath my wing.
> Close your eyes,
> My darlings,
> Let your cares drift away.
> Go to sleep, my sweethearts,
> Tomorrow is a brand-new day.

"What a lovely song," thought Mother Cow, and she too began to sing. To the farmer in his bed her song sounded like so much moo, moo, mooing.[1]

But her calf heard the music and understood the words. To him it was a beautiful lullaby that went like this:

> Come lie beside me
> Under stars so bright.
> Let dreams of shady pastures
> Bring on the morning light.
> Close your eyes, my darling,
> Let your cares drift away.
> Go to sleep, my sweetheart,
> Tomorrow is a brand-new day.[2]

"What a lovely song," thought Mother Horse, and she too began to sing. To the farmer in his bed her song sounded like so much neigh, neigh, neighing.

But her colt heard the music and understood the words. To him it was a beautiful lullaby that went like this:

> Tuck your legs beneath you,
> Legs that love to run.
> Feel them growing ever stronger.

Think Aloud

[1] *The little chicks understood Mother Hen's song, even if the farmer didn't. I wonder if Mother Cow's calf will understand her song in the same way?*

Think Aloud

[2] *I can picture in my mind what the little calf looks like as it settles down beside its mother because I've seen pictures of cows in books.*

Let the day be done.
Close your eyes, my darling,
Let your cares drift away.
Go to sleep, my sweetheart,
Tomorrow is a brand-new day.

"What a lovely song," thought Mother Pig, and she too began to sing. To the farmer in his bed her song sounded like so much oink, oink, oinking.

But her piglets heard the music and understood the words. To them it was a beautiful lullaby that went like this:

Wallowing in puddles,
Squealing with delight,
You've all had your mud bath,
Now it's time to say good night.
Close your eyes, my darlings,
Let your cares drift away.
Go to sleep, my sweethearts,
Tomorrow is a brand-new day.[3]

"What a lovely song," thought Mother Sheep, and she too began to sing. To the farmer in his bed her song sounded like so much baa, baa, baaing.

But her lamb heard the music and understood the words. To her it was a beautiful lullaby that went like this:

You danced in the clover,
While we grazed upon the hill.
Make my wool your pillow,
Let it keep you from the chill.
Close your eyes, my darling,
Let your cares drift away.
Go to sleep, my sweetheart,
Tomorrow is a brand-new day.

"Oh, what a lovely song," thought Mother Goose, and she too began to sing. To the farmer in his bed her song sounded like so much honk, honk, honking.

But her goslings heard the music and understood the words. To them it was a beautiful lullaby that went like this:

Waddle from the pond, dears,

Think Aloud

[3] *I think there is a pattern in this story. Each animal sings a lullaby that the farmer can't understand. I wonder if any other animals will start to sing.*

To our downy nest.
Swimming, dunking all the day,
Goslings need a rest.
Close your eyes, my darlings,
Let your cares drift away.
Go to sleep, my sweethearts,
Tomorrow is a brand-new day.

While the baby animals listened to their mothers' sweet voices, all the farmer heard was so much clucking and mooing and neighing and oinking and baaing and honking.

So he hollered out the window, "BE QUIET!"

But that only woke up his own baby, who started to cry. "WAAAAAAA!"[4]

"Now look what you've done!" grumbled the farmer's wife, and she began to sing:

Gentle breezes blowing
Softly in your hair.
Sounds of nighttime calling,
Music in the air.
Close your eyes, my darling,
Let your cares drift away.
Go to sleep, my sweetheart,
Tomorrow is a brand-new day.

To the animals in the barnyard her song was just so much noise. But the farmer heard the music and understood the words. To him it was a beautiful lullaby.

Think Aloud

[4] *I was able to picture in my mind the father sticking his head out the window to holler at all those noisy animals. I can imagine how the baby woke up screaming and crying, too, because my little brother does the same thing when he hears a loud noise.*

Retell the Story: Have the children act out the story. Assign roles of the people and animals.

Student Think Aloud

Use Copying Master number 1 to prompt children to share questions they had while listening to the story.

Think and Respond

1. How might you add another animal to this story? What might that animal be? *Possible response: I could have a spider whisper a lullaby to her baby spiders.* **Inferential**

2. Authors often include poems or songs in the middle of their stories. Why do you think this author did so? *Possible responses: He wanted to make the story more interesting; he wanted to show a pattern.* **Genre**

3. What do you think the author was trying to say about lullabies in this selection? *Possible response: Lullabies are sung by parents everywhere to soothe their children and help them sleep, no matter what the language.* **Author's Purpose**

THE GREAT KAPOK TREE
A TALE OF THE AMAZON RAIN FOREST

a fable
by Lynne Cherry

Genre: Fable
Comprehension Strategy: Generate Questions
Think-Aloud Copying Master number 1

Before Reading

Genre: Tell children that a fable is a short story that teaches a lesson. It often has animal characters that talk and act as people do. Some fables were created long ago, but others are quite new. Invite children to share the lessons they learned from other fables they have heard, such as "I Wish I Were a Butterfly" or "The Lion and the Mouse."

Expand Vocabulary: Introduce these words before reading:

Kapok tree: a rain-forest tree; one of the tallest trees in the South American rain forest

ancestors: animals or people who lived long ago

canopy: the tops of trees forming a kind of ceiling over the rain forest

understory: a layer of small trees and shrubs below the level of the taller trees in a rain forest

Set a Purpose for Reading: Have children listen to the selection and ask what happens to the man when he falls asleep under the kapok tree.

During Reading

Then use the Think Alouds during the first reading of the story. Notes about the genre and cultural perspective may be used during subsequent readings.

The Great Kapok Tree

A Tale of the Amazon Rain Forest

by Lynne Cherry

Two men walked into the rain forest. Moments before, the forest had been alive with the sounds of squawking birds and howling monkeys. Now all was quiet as the creatures watched the two men and wondered why they had come.

The larger man stopped and pointed to a great Kapok tree. Then he left.

The smaller man took the ax he carried and struck the trunk of the tree. Whack! Whack! Whack! The sounds of the blows rang through the forest. The wood of the tree was very hard. Chop! Chop! Chop! The man wiped off the sweat that ran down his face and neck. Whack! Chop! Whack! Chop!

Soon the man grew tired. He sat down to rest at the foot of the great Kapok tree. Before he knew it, the heat and hum of the forest had lulled him to sleep.

A boa constrictor lived in the Kapok tree. He slithered down its trunk to where the man was sleeping. He looked at the gash the ax had made in the tree. Then the huge snake slid very close to the man and hissed in his ear: "Senhor, this tree is a tree of miracles. It is my home, where generations of my ancestors have lived. Do not chop it down."

A bee buzzed in the sleeping man's ear: "Senhor, my hive is in this Kapok tree, and I fly from tree to tree and flower to flower collecting pollen. In this way I pollinate the trees and flowers throughout the rain forest. You see, all living things depend on one another."[1]

A troupe of monkeys scampered down from the canopy of the Kapok tree. They chattered to the sleeping man: "Senhor, we have seen the ways of man. You chop down one tree, then come back for another and another. The roots of these great trees will wither and die, and there will be nothing left to hold the earth in place. When the heavy rains come, the soil will be washed away and the forest will become a desert."

A toucan, a macaw, and a cock-of-the-rock flew down from the canopy. "Senhor!" squawked the toucan, "You must not cut

Think Aloud

[1]*I wonder if other animals will speak to the man. I'll keep listening to find out.*

Genre Study

Fable: A fable often has a lesson that is clearly stated at the end. In this fable, the lesson is expressed throughout the selection.

down this tree. We have flown over the rain forest and seen what happens once you begin to chop down the trees. Many people settle on the land. They set fires to clear the underbrush, and soon the forest disappears. Where once there was life and beauty only black and smoldering ruins remain."

A bright and small tree frog crawled along the edge of a leaf. In a squeaky voice he piped in the man's ear: "Senhor, a ruined rain forest means ruined lives . . . many ruined lives. You will leave many of us homeless if you chop down this great Kapok tree."[2]

A jaguar had been sleeping along a branch in the middle of the tree. Because his spotted coat blended into the dappled light and shadows of the understory, no one had noticed him. Now he leapt down and padded silently over to the sleeping man. He growled in his ear: "Senhor, the Kapok tree is home to many birds and animals. If you cut it down, where will I find my dinner?"

Four tree porcupines swung down from branch to branch and whispered to the man: "Senhor, do you know what we animals and humans need in order to live? Oxygen. And, Senhor, do you know what trees produce? Oxygen! If you cut down the forests you will destroy that which gives us all life."

Several anteaters climbed down the Kapok tree with their young clinging to their backs. The unstriped anteater said to the sleeping man: "Senhor, you are chopping down this tree with no thought for the future. And surely you know that what happens tomorrow depends upon what you do today. The big man tells you to chop down a beautiful tree. He does not think of his own children, who tomorrow must live in a world without trees."

A three-toed sloth had begun climbing down from the canopy when the men first appeared. Only now did she reach the ground. Plodding ever so slowly over to the sleeping man, she spoke in her deep and lazy voice: "Senhor, how much is beauty worth? Can you live without it? If you destroy the beauty of the rain forest, on what would you feast your eyes?"[3]

A child from the Yanomamo tribe who lived in the rain forest knelt over the sleeping man. He murmured in his ear: "Senhor, when you awake, please look upon us all with new eyes."

The man awoke with a start. Before him stood the rain forest child, and all around him, staring, were the creatures who

Think Aloud

[2]I wonder what the man would do if he woke up now. What would he say to the little frog?

Think Aloud

[3]I wonder what a three-toed sloth is. It must be an animal that lives in the rain forest since all the other things mentioned before this have been animals. From the description it sounds like the sloth is a lazy, slow-moving animal.

depended upon the great Kapok tree. What wondrous and rare animals they were![4]

The man looked about and saw the sun streaming through the canopy. Spots of bright light glowed like jewels amidst the dark green forest. Strange and beautiful plants seemed to dangle in the air, suspended from the great Kapok tree.

The man smelled the fragrant perfume of their flowers. He felt the steamy mist rising from the forest floor. But he heard no sound, for the creatures were strangely silent.

The man stood and picked up his ax. He swung back his arm as though to strike the tree. Suddenly he stopped. He turned and looked at the animals and the child.

He hesitated. Then he dropped the ax and walked out of the rain forest.

Think Aloud

[4]*I wonder if the man heard all that was whispered in his ear. If he did, I don't see how he could cut down the tree now. I sure couldn't!*

Retell the Story: Have children retell the story by acting it out. Assign the parts of the two men, boa constrictor, bee, troupe of monkeys, toucan, macaw, cock-of-the-rock, frog, jaguar, four porcupines, several anteaters, sloth, child, and narrator.

Student Think Aloud

Use Copying Master number 1 to prompt children to share any questions they had while listening to the story.

Cultural Perspective

Senhor is Portuguese for the word *sir* or *gentleman*. This language is spoken in Brazil where much of the Amazon rain forest is located.

Think and Respond

1. Why are living trees important? *Possible responses: Trees are homes to many animals; they provide oxygen which living things need to survive.* **Inferential**
2. How is this fable like others you have heard? *Possible response: It has animal characters that talk and it teaches a lesson.* **Genre**
3. What do you think the author wants you to learn from this story? *Possible responses: People should not cut down trees because they are valuable to people and animals. People should do things to help preserve and save the rain forests.* **Author's Purpose**

NAIL SOUP

a folktale

by Debi Gliori

Genre: Folktale

Comprehension Strategy: Visualize

Think-Aloud Copying Master number 3

Before Reading

Genre: Tell children that we do not usually know who first told folktales like the one they are about to hear. Folktales are passed from one person to another by word of mouth. Remind children of a similar folktale they have heard, "The Storytelling Stone."

Expand Vocabulary: Before reading, introduce these terms:

scrawny: very thin and bony

minuscule: tiny, extremely small

panting: taking short, fast breaths

scrumptious: having a very good taste, delicious

Set a Purpose for Reading: Have children listen to learn what happens when Fox goes to Hen's house for dinner.

During Reading

Then use the Think Alouds during the first reading of the story. The note about the genre may be used during subsequent readings.

NAIL SOUP

by Debi Gliori

Hen stood in her brand-new kitchen in her brand-new house and sighed. In front of her were six hundred and forty-two cardboard boxes full of her worldly goods. So far, she'd only unpacked one box and found her soup pot, her chopping board and knife and—would you believe it—one rusty nail.

The doorbell rang and a voice called, "Coo-eee! Anybody home?"

"My new neighbor," thought Hen, running to open the door. On the doorstep stood a large and scrawny fox.

"Good morning," he said. "Welcome to the neighborhood, my dear. I just thought I'd pop round to ask you over for dinner tonight."

Hen was about to reply when Fox grabbed her, slammed the door shut behind himself and growled, "Nothing too elaborrrrate—just you and me. You'll be the one simmerrring in the casserrrole, and I'll be the one with the knife and forrrk."[1]

Hen thought quickly—very quickly, as you do when you're about to be gobbled up.

"Dear Fox, I have a much better idea," she squawked. "Why don't you help me finish off my pot of nail soup? Seems a shame to waste a good soup when you're obviously so ravenous."[2]

"Nail soup?" said Fox. "Never heard of it."

"It's delicious," said Hen. "Now, why don't you unpack those boxes while I bring the soup to the boil?"

With a loud haaarrrrrurmph, he began to unpack the boxes. All six hundred and forty-two of them. Fox had just unpacked the last one when Hen brought him a spoonful of soup to taste.

"Bleurchhh!" he spat. "It's like hot, rusty water!"

"Mmm, you're quite right," murmured Hen. "Needs some salt to bring out the true nailishness of the soup. Tell you what, why don't you paint the living-room while I stir in the salt?"

Fox frowned. Something wasn't quite right here, but he didn't know what it was. Grumbling to himself he headed for the living-room.

He'd just put a final coat of gloss on the woodwork when Hen brought him another spoonful to try.

"Urrrchhhh!" he gagged. "Hot, rusty, salty water!"

Think Aloud

[1] *I can just picture this scene. Hen is expecting a friendly visit, and then Fox threatens to eat her! She probably looks scared and shocked.*

Think Aloud

[2] *I wonder what the word* ravenous *means. I will think about what clues I've heard. The fox wants to eat the hen. The hen talks about having the fox eat the soup, so I think* ravenous *means "hungry."*

"You could be right," mused Hen. "What we need are some root vegetables to give it some body . . . . Could you be troubled to put up my kitchen units while I chop and peel the vegetables?"

Fox slitted his eyes and glared at Hen, but then his tummy growled and he decided to humor her. Armed with a bent screwdriver and a set of instructions in Serbo-Croat, he set to work.

He was just admiring his handiwork when Hen brought him another spoonful.

"Mmmmm, much better," he said.

"But . . . ?" said Hen.

"Still a bit bland," said Fox.

"D'you know, I'm so glad you said that," said Hen. "I think so too. My instinct tells me that this soup needs a Mediterranean theme. Be a dear and sand the dining-room floor while I pick some beans and tomatoes for our soup."

Next time, vowed Fox, no matter what it tastes like, I'm eating it. He picked up a packet of minuscule nail files and headed for the dining-room.

Fox was lying panting in a corner of the freshly-sanded dining-room when Hen appeared with a spoonful of soup.

"Nearly there!" she said brightly, as the exhausted Fox took a sip. "Great," he wheezed. "Perfect. Let's have it n- . . ."[3]

"Now, now," chided Hen. "Don't rush it. Rome wasn't built in a day, you know. I still have to add some herbs and a wee bit of parmesan. Look, why don't you light the fire and we can eat by firelight?"

"Where's the wood?" groaned Fox.

"Growing on that big tree outside," said Hen, passing him a tiny axe.

The fire was blazing merrily and the Fox was nearly asleep beside it when Hen appeared with another spoonful.

"Delicious," yawned Fox. "I don't suppose . . .?"

"NO," said Hen firmly. "It needs to simmer a while to soften the nail thoroughly. While we wait, you can sew some curtains for that window, so we can eat our soup by the fire without having to look at the darkness outside."

Dumbly, the Fox picked up a needle and began to sew full-length-box-pleated-fully-lined curtains for Hen's window. Just as he'd finished and was pulling the curtains closed against the night, Hen arrived with a brimming pot of soup.

Genre Study

Folktale: This folktale is a trickster tale. In an unusual twist, the hen is the trickster and the fox is the one being tricked.

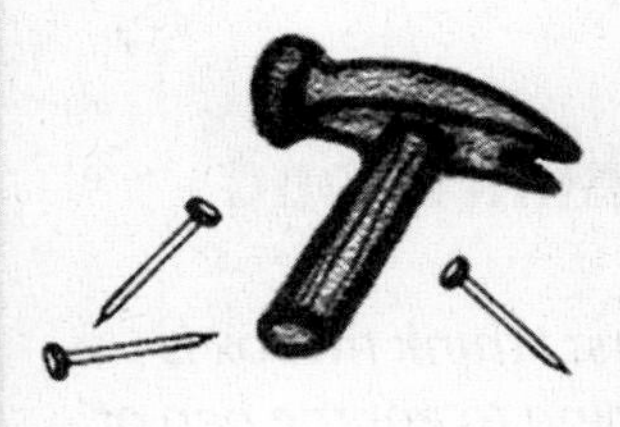

Think Aloud

[3] *I can picture Fox getting more and more tired. He is probably walking more slowly, while Hen looks happy and energetic as she cooks.*

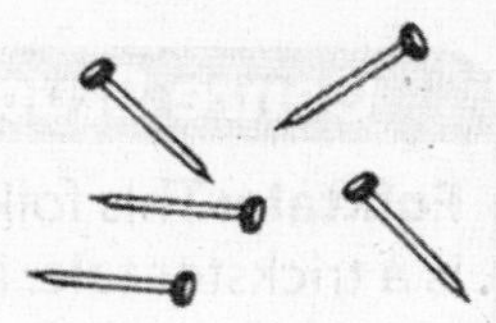

"Absolutely scrumptious!" said Fox, devouring his first bowl.

"Heaven in a pot!" he exclaimed after his third bowl.

"Who'd've thought a nail could taste this good?" he said, halfway through bowl eleven.

"Heavens, and so filling, too," he gasped after bowl twenty-eight.

"I couldn't possibly manage another spoonful," he groaned as he emptied the pot.

"Oh well," said Hen with a wide grin. "Then it must be time for you to eat me." She sat back in her armchair by the fire, safe in the knowledge that the fox was far too full to eat anything more.

Aware that he'd been totally outfoxed, Fox looked at Hen, gave a huge belch, and with a furious roar, ran howling through the front door.[4]

And was never seen again.

Think Aloud

[4] *First I think the fox is going to eat the hen at some point in the story. But then I find out that he is too full from eating the soup, so he can't eat the hen.*

Retell the Story: Have children create paper puppets of the fox and the hen. Then have them use the puppets to retell the story.

Student Think Aloud

Use Copying Master number 3 to prompt children to visualize a favorite part of the story.

"I was able to picture in my mind . . ."

Think and Respond

1. Do you think it was good or bad that the hen tricked the fox? Why? *Possible response: Good because the fox was going to eat the hen. She saved herself by tricking him.* **Critical**
2. What does Hen do that shows she is the trickster in this folktale? *Possible responses: She tricks the fox into doing things around her house, then she makes the fox eat so much soup that he is too full to eat Hen.* **Genre**
3. What do you think is the author's message? *Possible response: People can outsmart others to protect themselves.* **Author's Purpose**

This Is Our Earth

a poem
by Laura Lee Benson

Genre: Poem
Poetic Element: Rhyme
Comprehension Strategy: Generate Questions
Think-Aloud Copying Master number 1

Before Reading

Genre: Tell children that a rhyming poem contains a rhyming pattern. Rhyming words may be used at the end of each line, every other line, or sometimes in a more complex pattern. Explain that this particular poem when set to music is also a song.

Expand Vocabulary: Before reading, introduce these terms:

cherish: to value something highly

terrain: land or countryside

preserve: to keep something protected; to make sure it lasts

Set a Purpose for Reading: Have children listen for the rhyming words.

During Reading

Read through the poem the first time without interruptions. Then reread, using the Think Aloud and genre note.

This Is Our Earth

by Laura Lee Benson

I
This is our Earth to cherish and love
To clean and protect, to take care of
From the mountains so high with their rugged terrain
To the valleys below and the green grassy plain,
This is our Earth.

II
From the tall wooded forests with their towering trees
To the fish, whales, and dolphins that live in the seas
From the deserts of sand where the tall cactus grow
To the cold Arctic north with its glaciers and snow,
This is our Earth.

III
From the rain forests where the wild parrot calls
Near the swift flowing rivers and lush waterfalls
To the wide open prairies where elk can be found
And thousands of prairie dogs that live underground,
This is our Earth.

IV
From the shimmering lakes where flocks of geese swim
And the blue jay keeps watch from a lofty tree limb
To the farms in the country where cows graze on hay
And the parks in the cities where children play,
This is our Earth.

V
So take a good look and I think you will find
That this beautiful Earth is one of a kind.
Let's do our share to lend a hand
To preserve all we have in this wonderful land,
This is our Earth.[1]

VI
This is our Earth to cherish and love
To clean and protect, to take care of
This is our Earth to cherish and love
To clean and protect from below and above,
This is our Earth.

Genre Study

Poem: There are different rhyming patterns used in poems. In this poem, the first two lines in each verse rhyme and the third and fourth lines rhyme.

Think Aloud

[1] *I wonder if this poem will make people realize how important it is to take care of Earth and protect all the animals on it. I know that now I'll think more carefully about how I might keep our planet healthy.*

Retell the Poem: Have children draw a picture of a favorite part of the poem and describe it using rhyming words, if possible.

Student Think Aloud

Use Copying Master number 1 to prompt children to think of something they would like to ask the author.

Think and Respond

1. How does this poem make you feel? *Responses will vary. Possible response: It makes me feel like I need to help preserve Earth.* **Critical**
2. What words help you to picture the scenes in this poem? *Possible responses: tall wooded forests, towering trees, arctic north with its glaciers and snow* **Genre**
3. What is the poet's purpose for writing this poem? What message do you think she wanted to share with her readers? *Possible response: She wants to tell people to help clean and protect Earth.* **Author's Purpose**

Cloudy With a Chance of Meatballs

a fantasy

by Judi Barrett

Genre: Fantasy

Comprehension Strategy: Visualize

Think-Aloud Copying Master number 3

Before Reading

Genre: Explain to children that fantasy is fiction that contains characters, settings, and events that are not realistic. In this selection, it rains food instead of water.

Expand Vocabulary: Introduce the following words before reading:

varied: included many different forms or kinds

abandon: to leave a place because of danger

stale: no longer fresh

Set a Purpose for Reading: Have children listen to find out what happens to a town where it rains food.

During Reading

Use the Think Alouds during the first reading of the story. Notes about the genre and cultural perspective may be used during subsequent readings.

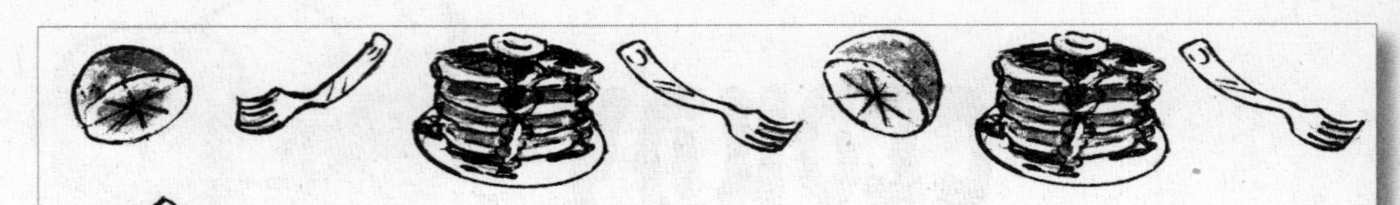

Cloudy With a Chance of Meatballs

by Judi Barrett

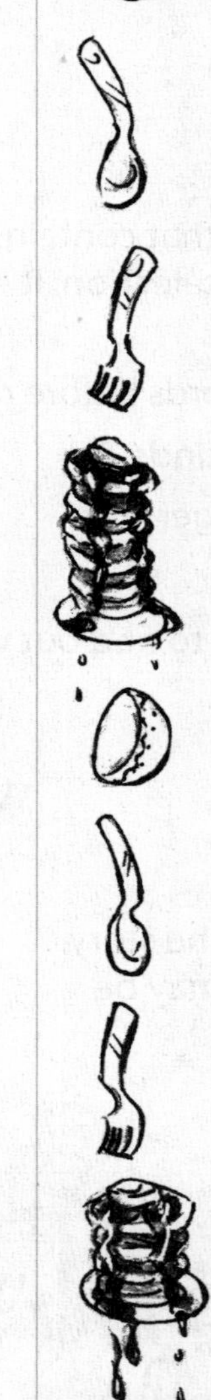

We were all sitting around the big kitchen table. It was Saturday morning. Pancake morning. Mom was squeezing oranges for juice. Henry and I were betting on how many pancakes we each could eat. And Grandpa was doing the flipping.

Seconds later, something flew through the air headed toward the kitchen ceiling . . .

. . . and landed right on Henry.

After we realized that the flying object was only a pancake, we all laughed, even Grandpa. Breakfast continued quite uneventfully. All the other pancakes landed in the pan. And all of them were eaten, even the one that landed on Henry.

That night, touched off by the pancake incident at breakfast, Grandpa told us the best tall-tale bedtime story he'd ever told.

"Across an ocean, over lots of huge bumpy mountains, across three hot deserts, and one smaller ocean . . .

. . . there lay the tiny town of Chewandswallow.[1]

In most ways, it was very much like any other tiny town. It had a Main Street lined with stores, houses with trees and gardens around them, a schoolhouse, about three hundred people, and some assorted cats and dogs.

But there were no food stores in the town of Chewandswallow. They didn't need any. The sky supplied all the food they could possibly want.

The only thing that was really different about Chewandswallow was its weather. It came three times a day, at breakfast, lunch, and dinner. Everything that everyone ate came from the sky.

Whatever the weather served, that was what they ate.

But it never rained rain. It never snowed snow. And it never blew just wind. It rained things like soup and juice. It snowed mashed potatoes and green peas. And sometimes the wind blew in storms of hamburgers.

Think Aloud

[1] I've never heard of a town called Chewandswallow! It sounds like "chew and swallow." I think this is the beginning of the fantasy story that Grandpa told them that night.

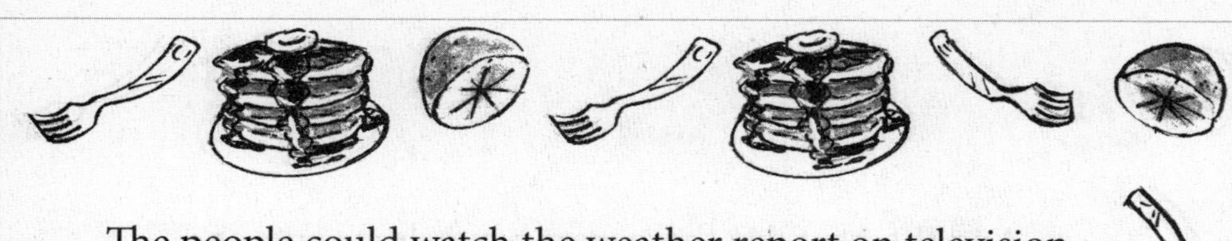

The people could watch the weather report on television in the morning and they would hear a prediction for the next day's food.

When the townspeople went outside, they carried their plates, cups, glasses, forks, spoons, knives and napkins with them. That way they would always be prepared for any kind of weather.

If there were left-overs, and there usually were, the people took them home and put them in their refrigerators in case they got hungry between meals.

The menu varied.

By the time they woke up in the morning, breakfast was coming down.

After a brief shower of orange juice, low clouds of sunny-side up eggs moved in followed by pieces of toast. Butter and jelly sprinkled down for the toast. And most of the time it rained milk afterwards.

For lunch one day, frankfurters, already in their rolls, blew in from the northwest at about five miles an hour.

There were mustard clouds nearby. Then the wind shifted to the east and brought in baked beans.

A drizzle of soda finished off the meal.

Dinner one night consisted of lamb chops, becoming heavy at times, with occasional ketchup. Periods of peas and baked potatoes were followed by gradual clearing, with a wonderful Jell-O setting in the west.[2]

The Sanitation Department of Chewandswallow had a rather unusual job for a sanitation department. It had to remove the food that fell on the houses and sidewalks and lawns. The workers cleaned things up after every meal and fed all the dogs and cats. Then they emptied some of it into the surrounding oceans for the fish and turtles and whales to eat. The rest of the food was put back into the earth so that the soil would be richer for the people's flower gardens.

Life for the townspeople was delicious until the weather took a turn for the worse.

One day there was nothing but Gorgonzola cheese all day long.

The next day there was only broccoli, all overcooked.

Genre Study

Fantasy: A humorous fantasy is a story that has humorous or funny events that could not really happen. The idea of people carrying around plates to catch their dinner is a humorous sight.

Think Aloud

[2] *I notice the author is describing meals like a weather report I would hear on the nightly news! This makes this strange town's weather seem very funny.*

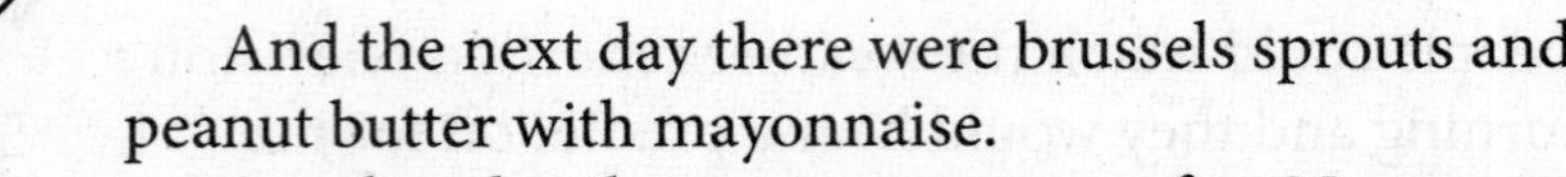

And the next day there were brussels sprouts and peanut butter with mayonnaise.

Another day there was a pea soup fog. No one could see where they were going and they could barely find the rest of the meal that got stuck in the fog.

The food was getting larger and larger, and so were the portions. The people were getting frightened. Violent storms blew up frequently. Awful things were happening.

One Tuesday there was a hurricane of bread and rolls all day long and into the night. There were soft rolls and hard rolls, some with seeds and some without. There was white bread and rye and whole wheat toast. Most of it was larger than they had ever seen bread and rolls before. It was a terrible day. Everyone had to stay indoors. Roofs were damaged, and the Sanitation Department was beside itself. The mess took the workers four days to clean up, and the sea was full of floating rolls.

To help out, the people piled up as much bread as they could in their backyards. The birds kept at it a bit, but it just stayed there and got staler and staler.

There was a storm of pancakes one morning and a downpour of maple syrup that nearly flooded the town. A huge pancake covered the school. No one could get it off because of its weight, so they had to close the school.

Lunch one day brought fifteen-inch drifts of cream cheese and jelly sandwiches. Everyone ate themselves sick and the day ended with a stomachache.

There was an awful salt and pepper wind accompanied by an even worse tomato tornado. People were sneezing themselves silly and running to avoid the tomatoes. The town was a mess. There were seeds and pulp everywhere.[3]

The Sanitation Department gave up. The job was too big.

Everyone feared for their lives. They couldn't go outside most of the time. Many houses had been badly damaged by giant meatballs, stores were boarded up and there was no more school for the children.

So a decision was made to abandon the town of Chewandswallow.

Think Aloud

[3]*I was able to picture in my mind the mess this town is in. I know how squishy tomatoes can be, so I can imagine what a mess a whole tornado-worth of them would make!*

It was a matter of survival.

The people glued together the giant pieces of stale bread sandwich-style with peanut butter . . .

. . . took the absolute necessities with them, and set sail on their rafts for a new land.

After being afloat for a week, they finally reached a small coastal town, which welcomed them. The bread had held up surprisingly well, well enough for them to build temporary houses for themselves out of it.

The children began school again, and the adults all tried to find places for themselves in the new land. The biggest change they had to make was getting used to buying food at a supermarket. They found it odd that the food was kept on shelves, packaged in boxes, cans and bottles. Meat that had to be cooked was kept in large refrigerators. Nothing came down from the sky except rain and snow. The clouds above their heads were not made of fried eggs. No one ever got hit by a hamburger again.

And nobody dared to go back to Chewandswallow to find out what had happened to it. They were too afraid."

Henry and I were awake until the very end of Grandpa's story. I remember his good-night kiss.

The next morning we woke up to see snow falling outside our window.

We ran downstairs for breakfast and ate it a little faster than usual so we could go sledding with Grandpa.

It's funny, but even as we were sliding down the hill we thought we saw a giant pat of butter at the top, and we could almost smell mashed potatoes.

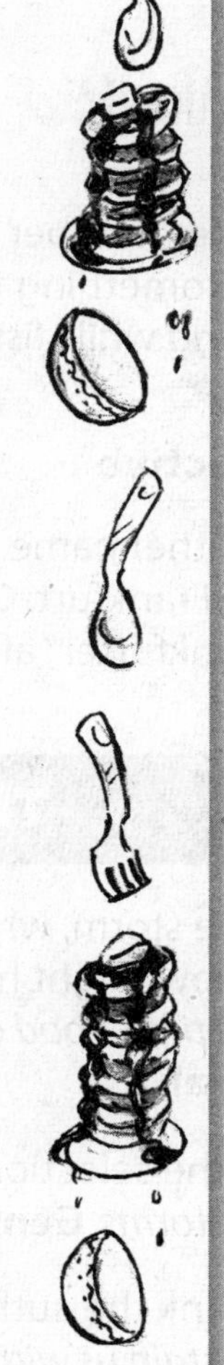

After Reading

Retell the Story: Ask children to draw a picture of it raining in Chewandswallow. Then have them draw a picture of Chewandswallow when the violent storms occurred. Invite children to explain their drawings to retell the events of the story.

Student Think Aloud

"I was able to picture in my mind . . ."

Use Copying Master number 3 to prompt children to share something they were able to picture in their mind while listening to the story.

Cultural Perspective

Frankfurters is another name for hot dogs. In the 1800s the butcher's guild in Frankfurt, Germany, introduced a sausage and called it a "frankfurter" after their hometown.

Think and Respond

1. Even before the storm, what kinds of trouble do you think the people of Chewandswallow might have had? *Possible responses: They had a lot of food to clean up all the time. Food could fall on people's clothes and heads and get them dirty.* **Inferential**
2. What parts of the selection tell you it is a fantasy? *Possible response: the falling food and food storms* **Genre**
3. Why do you think the author told this story? *Possible responses: I think she wanted to entertain us with a funny story. She wanted to show how you can use your imagination.* **Author's Purpose**

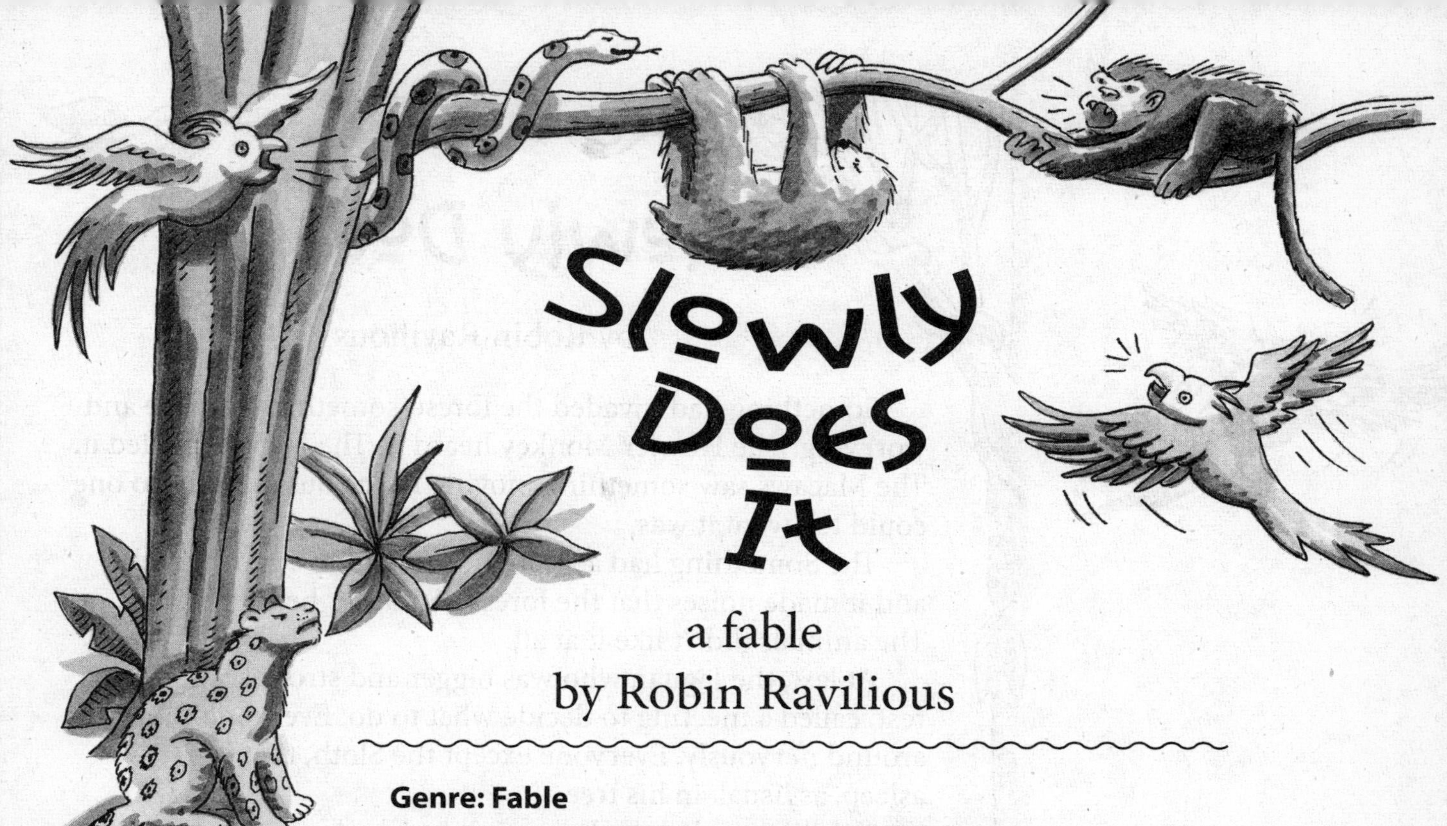

Slowly Does It

a fable

by Robin Ravilious

Genre: Fable

Comprehension Strategy: Adjust Reading Rate

Think-Aloud Copying Master number 7

Before Reading

Genre: Remind children that a fable is a story that teaches a lesson. It usually has animals that speak as if they are humans. The characters in this selection are rain-forest animals. Ask children to think of other fables they have heard, such as "The Great Kapok Tree" and "I Wish I Were a Butterfly."

Expand Vocabulary: Before reading, introduce these terms:

snarling: growling

rumpus: a disturbance

helter-skelter: a hurried or disorganized situation

hobgoblin: a make-believe thing that causes fear

Set a Purpose for Reading: Have children listen to the story to find out what the title means.

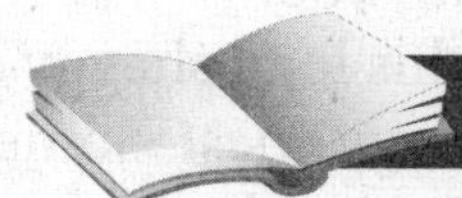

During Reading

Use the Think Alouds during the first reading of the story. Notes about the genre and cultural perspective may be used during subsequent readings.

Slowly Does It

by Robin Ravilious

Something had invaded the forest; something strange and worrying. The Howler Monkey heard it. The Jaguar smelled it. The Macaws saw something moving in the bushes. But no one could tell what it was.

The Something had a strange smell; it left strange tracks; and it made noises that the forest had never heard before. The animals didn't like it at all.

At last, the Jaguar, who was bigger and stronger than the rest, called a meeting to decide what to do. Everyone gathered around nervously. Everyone except the Sloth, that is. He was asleep, as usual, in his tree.

"Well!" growled the Jaguar in his deep fierce voice. "Does anyone know what this Something is?"

"It's much taller than a monkey," said the Howler Monkey.

"It has a shiny yellow head," said a Macaw.

"It makes a terrible snarling noise," said a Marmoset. "But sometimes it whistles like a bird."

"It smells bad, like fire," said a Snake. Then the Jaguar asked the question they were most worried about. "What does it *eat*?"

The animals looked at each other in silence. No one knew what it ate. They just hoped it ate nothing but fruit. The fact was that no one had seen it properly at all.[1]

Then the Jaguar had an idea.

"What about that good-for-nothing Sloth?" he growled. "He's been hanging about for weeks. He must have seen it. Go and call the Sloth."

Everyone looked up, and there, high above them in the tallest tree, was a dirty-looking bundle of hair hanging from a branch. The Howler Monkey went tearing up.

"Hey, you! Slowpoke!" he yelled, shaking the Sloth's branch. "Shift your bulk. Jaguar wants a word with you."

The Sloth was hanging peacefully by his long shaggy arms and legs, with his head resting on his shaggy chest. Sometimes he ate the leaves he could reach. Mostly he just hung there, fast asleep. He had hung so still for so long that green mold was

Think Aloud

[1]*There are many characters in this story and they are all giving clues about who invaded the forest. I will make sure to read slowly so I don't miss any clues.*

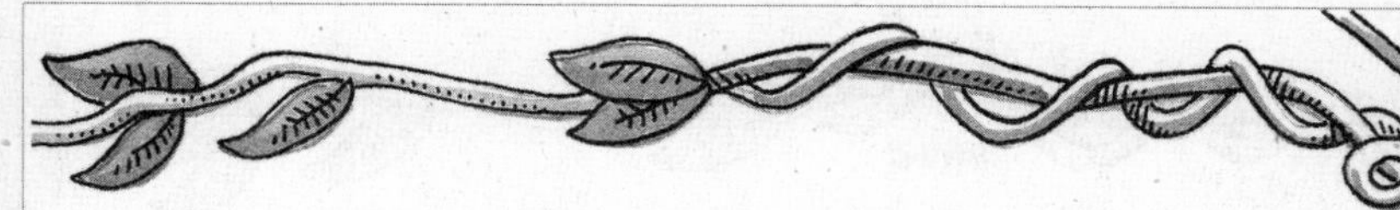

growing is his hair. He took no notice whatever of the Howler Monkey.

The Howler Monkey shouted and bounced until fruit rained down on the animals below, but the Sloth slept on.

Then all the little Marmosets went scampering up to try waking him. "Quick, quick, quick!" they chattered, jumping from twig to twig like grasshoppers.

The Sloth opened his short-sighted eyes. Then he shut them again.

The Tree Snake went next, coiling and twisting up the tree, and out along the branch.

"I sshould sstop thiss ssnoozing," he whispered in the Sloth's ear. "Better ssafe than ssorry."

The Sloth just opened his mouth in a long, slow-motion yawn.

Then the Macaws had a go. They flew around and around the Sloth, flashing their bright wings and squawking fit to choke.

"Wake up, Slug-a-bed, WAKE UP! Jaguar wants to talk."

The Sloth unhooked one arm and scratched his tummy drowsily.

Then the Jaguar lost his temper. He leaped and clawed his way up the tree, lashing his tail with rage.

"Look here, you moldy old hammock," he roared. "Are you going to talk, or do I have to make you?"

The Sloth peered at his visitor. "Good . . . morning," he said slowly (although it was afternoon by now). "What . . . seems . . . to . . . be . . . the . . . trouble?"

All the animals burst out talking at once: growling, yelling, hissing, chattering and squawking about the Something. The Sloth just hung there smiling, and slowly blinking his eyes.

The rumpus went on for some time, for the Sloth wasn't very bright. It took a while to get a new idea into his shaggy head.

"A . . . Something?" he said at last. "What . . . sort . . . of . . ."

"Stop!" interrupted the Howler Monkey. "Listen!"

Everyone went quiet. Up from the ground far beneath them came a noise more terrifying than anything they had ever heard before. An ugly, ear-splitting snarling roar it was, and it filled them with fear. Then there was a loud crack, a huge

Genre Study

Fable: Animals in fables often act and talk as people do. The talking animals in this fable react to the laziness of the Sloth as real people would. They try to wake him up in both rough and gentle ways.

crash, and one of the nearby trees just . . . fell down.

The animals could not believe their eyes.

"The Something," whispered the Jaguar, with his fur standing on end. "It's eating the trees."

At that, they all fled in panic, tumbling helter-skelter through the branches to get away. In a moment, they were all gone. All except the Sloth, of course. He was left hanging there alone, with his mouth open, and his question unanswered.

"Nobody . . . tells . . . me . . . anything," he sighed. "I . . . s'pose . . . I'd . . . better . . . go . . . and . . . see . . ."

Then, at last, he started to move. Inch by inch, he crept along his branch until he reached the main trunk. The awful noise went on and on, but he took no notice. He wrapped his shaggy arms around the tree and began to climb down. Slowly—oh, so slowly—he groped his way down, and down . . . and down. It was growing dark under the trees, and the noise had stopped, but still he toiled on. He was nearly there, and feeling so tired, when into the clearing came . . . the Something. They stared at each other.

What the Sloth saw was a man. A man with a chainsaw for cutting down trees.[2] But the Sloth didn't know it was a man. He'd never met one before. He peered at it doubtfully. Then he did what sloths always do to stay out of trouble: he kept quite still and smiled.

But what the man saw, however, in that shadowy forest, far from home, was a horrible hairy hobgoblin leering at him with a spooky grin on its face. It made his blood run cold. He let out a strangled cry, and ran for his life.[3]

Next morning, the other animals came anxiously creeping back. They sniffed the air for that frightening smell. They listened for the frightening noise. But all they smelled were sweet forest scents; and all they heard were the friendly forest calls. The Something had gone. And there was the Sloth dangling from his branch in the sunshine, and slowly stuffing leaves into his smile.

Think Aloud

[2]There were hints in this story all along that the Something was a man with a chainsaw. Chainsaws make a snarling sound and can smell like fire. And they really do seem to eat trees when they cut them down. I am glad I read carefully so I could think about the clues.

Think Aloud

[3]What does "it made his blood run cold" mean? The man sees a horrible, hairy thing with a spooky grin. The man must be scared because he runs away. I think "it made his blood run cold" means something frightened him.

Retell the Story: Have children fold a sheet of paper in thirds. Ask them to draw a picture of what happened in the beginning, a picture of what happened in the middle, and a picture of what happened at the end. Have them use their pictures to retell the story.

Student Think Aloud

"This was mostly about . . ."

Use Copying Master number 7 to prompt children to summarize the selection.

Cultural Perspective

Rain forests have a bigger variety of trees than any other area in the world. Many trees and plants in a rain forest can be used for food and medicines without destroying them. But if the trees are cut down, these useful purposes are lost.

Think and Respond

1. How might the story be different if the sloth did not look for the Something? *Possible response: The man might have stayed in the forest and cut down more trees.* **Analytical**

2. How is this fable similar to "The Lion and the Mouse"? How is it different? *Possible response: There are talking animals and it has a lesson. In "The Lion and the Mouse," friends learned about helping. In this story, we learn about how man's actions affect Earth.* **Genre**

3. What do you think the author is trying to show in this story? *Possible response: That the slower, weaker ones can be the heroes.* **Author's Purpose**

THE DESERT IS THEIRS

a poem
by Byrd Baylor

Genre: Poem

Poetic Element: Imagery

Comprehension Strategy: Generate Questions

Think-Aloud Copying Master number 1

Before Reading

Genre: Tell children that some poems do not have rhyming words. These poems use certain words to create thoughts and feelings in the reader. Remind children of another poem they have heard, "This Is Our Earth." Explain that you will read a poem about the desert.

Expand Vocabulary: Introduce the following desert words before reading:

adobe: brick made from earth and straw

Papagos: members of a Native North American tribe

Yucca: an evergreen plant

Saguaro: a large cactus

Set a Purpose for Reading: Invite children to visualize the desert's plants and animals as they listen to the poem.

During Reading

Read through the poem the first time without interruptions. Then reread the poem again and pause to draw children's attention to the Think Aloud and genre note. Ask children to pay attention to words that help them see, hear, smell, taste, or feel the things in the desert.

THE DESERT IS THEIRS

by Byrd Baylor

The desert gives
what it can
to each of its children.[1]
Women weave grass
into their baskets
and birds weave it into their nests.

Men dig
in the earth
for soil
to make houses—
little square adobe houses
the color of the hills.
And lizards
dig burrows
in the same
safe earth.

Here animals and people know
what plants to eat
when they are sick.
They know what roots
and weeds
can make them well again.

No one has to tell
Coyote or Deer
and no one has to tell
the Papagos.
They share in other ways too.
They share
the feeling
of being
brothers
in the desert,
of being
desert creatures
together.

Think Aloud

[1] *I have many questions about this beginning. I wonder what a desert can give. I wonder who the desert's children are.*

Genre Study

Poem: A poem that doesn't follow a set form and does not have a standard length of lines is written in free verse. Free verse poems also do not have to rhyme.

A year that is hard
for people
is hard for
scorpions too.
It's hard for everything.

Rain is a blessing
counted
drop
by
drop.
Each plant
finds its own way
to hold
that sudden water.
They don't waste it
on floppy green leaves.
They have thorns
and stickers
and points
instead.[2]

Yucca
sends roots searching
far far underground—
farther than you'd ever
dream
a root
would go.

And Saguaro is fat
after rain—
fat with the water
it's saving
inside its great stem.
Give it one summer storm.
It can last a year
if it has to.
Sometimes it has to.[3]

The desert's children
learn to be patient.

Think Aloud

[2] I wonder how all of the living things in the desert get enough water.

Think Aloud

[3] I can picture in my mind a thirsty desert using up every drop of water from the rain. The poet creates this picture with the words she chooses.

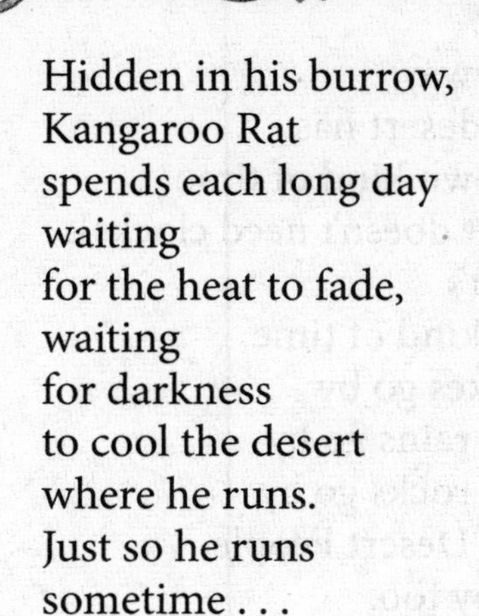

Hidden in his burrow,
Kangaroo Rat
spends each long day
waiting
for the heat to fade,
waiting
for darkness
to cool the desert
where he runs.
Just so he runs
sometime . . .

A weed
may wait
three years
to bloom.
Just so it blooms
sometime . . .

A toad
may wait
for months
to leave
his sandy hiding place
and sing toad songs
after a rain.
Just so he sings
sometime . . .

Desert people
are patient too.
You don't see them
rushing.
You don't hear them
shouting.[4]

They say you plant
happier corn
if you take your time
and that squash tastes best
if you've sung it
slow songs
while it's growing.
They do.

Think Aloud

[4]This was mostly about how patiently desert plants, animals, and people wait for the rain, and how they are very careful not to waste even a drop.

Anyway,
the desert has
its own kind of time
(that doesn't need clocks).
That's
the kind of time
snakes go by
and rains go by
and rocks go by
and Desert People
go by too.

That's why
every desert thing
knows
when the time comes
to celebrate.

Suddenly . . .
All together.
It happens.

Cactus blooms
yellow and pink and
purple.
The Papagos begin
their ceremonies
to pull down
rain.
Every plant joins in.
Even the dry earth
makes a sound of joy
when the rain touches.
Hawks call across the
canyons.
Children laugh for
nothing.
Coyotes dance in the
moonlight.

Where else
would
Desert People
want to be?

Retell: Have children visualize and then draw a picture of something described in the poem. Have them describe their pictures.

Student Think Aloud

"I wonder . . ."

Use Copying Master number 1 to prompt children to share questions they had while listening to the poem.

Cultural Perspective

The name *Papagos* means "desert people" or "bean people." The Papagos grow beans as well as corn and squash in the desert.

Think and Respond

1. What would it be like to be an animal or plant in the desert? *Possible responses: It would be difficult. You would need to be patient, share food and other things, and have strength to survive.* **Inferential**
2. Poems often create images or pictures in your mind. What picture does this poem create? *Possible responses: desert people making baskets and homes; cactus blooming; coyotes dancing* **Genre**
3. What might the author want you to learn about the desert? *Responses will vary. Possible response: The desert is a hard place to live, but the animals, plants, and people who live there are happy.* **Author's Purpose**

Albert's Play

a poem

by Leslie Tryon

Genre: Narrative Poem

Poetic Element: Rhyme and Rhythmic Pattern

Comprehension Strategy: Visualize

Think-Aloud Copying Master number 3

Before Reading

Genre: Tell children that a narrative poem is a poem that tells a story. It combines storytelling and poetry. Narrative poems are appealing to the listener because of the use of strong rhyme and repetition to create rhythmical sounds and patterns.

Expand Vocabulary: Introduce these words before reading:

runcible spoon: a sharp-edged fork having three broad prongs

shilling: an old English coin

mince: small, chopped bits of meat

quince: a fruit

Set a Purpose for Reading: Have children listen to the selection for rhyming words. Ask them to visualize the preparation for a play based on an old poem.

During Reading

Read through the poem the first time without interruptions and emphasizing the rhythm and cadence of the poem. Reread the poem again and pause to discuss the Think Aloud and genre note.

Albert's Play

by Leslie Tryon

It's time for that yearly tradition,
  The production of Albert's play.
Will children who wish to audition
  Be on stage after school today!

As soon as Albert had picked out the cast,
  He set the crew into motion.
They began with a tub and a flagpole mast,
  And they painted the blue of the ocean.
The stars, the moon, the bongs, and the boat—
  There were too many things to do!
Posters to draw, and boxes to tote,
  And learning to dance on cue,
    On cue,
    On cue,
  And learning to dance on cue.

They dangled the stars and the dancing moon
  While working faster and faster.
No one had yet found a runcible spoon—
  This could be a disaster!
There were masks to make too, to cut, and to glue.
  Would they ever get everything done?
Rehearsal was called for half-past two.
  Who said doing a play would be fun,
    Be fun,
    Be fun?
  Who said doing a play would be fun?

Albert fixed the lights and wiped some tears.
  They rehearsed until it was right.
He soothed those last-minute jitters and fears,
  And said, "You'll be fine by tonight."
They put on their costumes, practiced a bow,
  Albert double-checked every detail.
The theater is full—Shhhh! it's just minutes now,
  Till the Owl and the Pussy-cat sail,
    Set sail,
    Set sail,
 Till the Owl and the Pussy-cat sail.[1]

Think Aloud

[1] *I was able to picture in my mind how busy everyone was making scenery and practicing for the play because my class put on a play and everyone worked very hard.*

Genre Study

Poem: This poem also uses personification. The writer makes the animals speak and act like people.

Ladies and Gentleman . . .

The Owl and the Pussy-cat

by Edward Lear

The Owl and the Pussy-cat went to sea
In a beautiful pea-green boat,
They took some honey, and plenty of money,
Wrapped up in a five-pound note.
The Owl looked up to the stars above,
And sang to a small guitar,
'O lovely Pussy! O Pussy, my love,
What a beautiful Pussy you are,
You are,
You are!
What a beautiful Pussy you are!'[2]

Pussy said to the Owl, 'You elegant fowl!
How charmingly sweet you sing!
O let us be married! Too long we have tarried:
But what shall we do for a ring?'
They sailed away, for a year and a day,
To the land where the Bong-tree grows
And there in a wood a Piggy-wig stood
With a ring at the end of his nose,
His nose,
His nose,
With a ring at the end of his nose.

'Dear Pig, are you willing to sell for one <u>shilling</u>
Your ring?' Said the Piggy, 'I will.'
So they took it away, and were married next day
By the Turkey who lives on the hill.
They dined on <u>mince</u>, and slices of <u>quince</u>,
Which they ate with a runcible spoon;
And hand in hand, on the edge of the sand,
They danced by the light of the moon,
The moon,
The moon,
They danced by the light of the moon.

Think Aloud

[2]I was able to picture in my mind the Owl and the Pussycat by the words the poet used to describe their boat trip. I can imagine the cat purring as the Owl sings to her.

After Reading

Retell: Have children visualize a part from "The Owl and the Pussy-cat," and draw a picture of it. Have them describe their pictures using rhyming words.

Student Think Aloud

Use Copying Master number 3 to prompt children to share something that they visualized in the poem.

"I was able to picture in my mind . . ."

Cultural Perspective

Edward Lear was a British poet and painter who was known for his humorous poems. Lear became famous for his short rhymed verses called *limericks.*

Think and Respond

1. The play in this poem is described as "Albert's play." Who is Albert? *Possible responses: Albert is probably a teacher at school. He is the person in charge of the play.* **Inferential**
2. What makes this poem fun to hear? *Possible responses: the rhythm, humor, rhyming words* **Genre**
3. What do you think was the poet's purpose for writing this poem? *Possible responses: to entertain; to tell a story about preparing for a play and sharing the actual play* **Author's Purpose**

LEWIS AND CLARK:

A PRAIRIE DOG FOR THE PRESIDENT

by Shirley Raye Redmond

Genre: Nonfiction/Expository
Comprehension Strategy: Summarize
Think-Aloud Copying Master number 4

Before Reading

Genre: Remind children that nonfiction selections are ones that contain true facts used to inform the reader about a topic or event. Invite children to recall other nonfiction selections they have heard, such as "Police Patrol."

Expand Vocabulary: Before reading, introduce these terms:

explorer: somebody who travels to previously unknown places

scouts: people who can find paths through unexplored land

rodent: a small mammal, such as a mouse, rat, or squirrel

stagecoach: a large, four-wheeled coach pulled by a horse

Set a Purpose for Reading: Have children listen to the selection to discover how President Jefferson got a prairie dog.

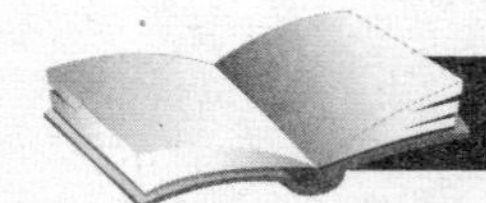

During Reading

Use the Think Alouds during the first reading of the selection. Notes about the genre and cultural perspective may be used during subsequent readings.

Lewis and Clark: A Prairie Dog for the President

by Shirley Raye Redmond

In 1803, Thomas Jefferson was the president of the United States.

The country was still new. It was also *very* big! It was so big no one had ever explored it all. President Jefferson wondered how long it would take to reach the Pacific Ocean. He wondered what the land was like along the way.

The president wrote to his friend Meriwether Lewis. Lewis was a soldier. He wanted to be an explorer. Lewis's buddy William Clark wanted to be an explorer too.

Lewis and Clark went to see the president. "I need someone to explore the West," said the president. "We'll do it!" said Lewis and Clark.

The president told Lewis and Clark to make maps and explore rivers. He told them to collect plants and draw wild animals. Most important, he told them to send presents!

Lewis and Clark needed helpers for their journey. They took soldiers, scouts, and boatmen. Lewis even took his dog. It was a *long* trip. One of the scouts brought his wife, Sacagawea (sack-uh-juh-WEE-uh).

Sacagawea was a big help. She picked nuts and berries. She cooked meat and stew. She talked and traded with the Indians they met on the way.[1]

Out west, Lewis and Clark made maps. They explored rivers. They collected plants.

They saw animals they had never seen before. They saw buffalo. They saw grizzly bears. They saw jackrabbits with long ears. They drew pictures of the animals.

They tried to catch some of the animals to send to the president. But the buffalo were too big. The grizzly bears were too dangerous. The jackrabbits were too fast. "The president will think we've forgotten him," they worried.

One day, Lewis and Clark came to a prairie. The ground was filled with holes. A little animal sat by each hole. "What are those?" asked Lewis.

Think Aloud

[1] I figured out that Sacagawea must be a Native American because of the way her name sounds and because the story mentions she talks to the Indians. She must know how to speak the same language if she talks to them.

Just then a hawk flew overhead. The little animals barked. Then they dived into their holes. "Let's catch one of those rascals," Clark said. "They are small enough to send to the president."[2]

The soldiers took shovels and picks. They dug and dug. But the little animals were too fast.

"Let's flood them out," Lewis said. The men carried water from the river. Lewis poured the water into a hole. Clark and the soldiers waited beside the other holes. They waited and waited and waited.

Then one of the animals popped up. "I've got it!" said Clark. Clark put the animal in a cage.

"I wonder what it is?" he said. Lewis laughed, "It is a wet rodent! You can call it a ground rat." "No," said Clark. "It looks like a squirrel. I'll call it a barking squirrel."

"Squirrels don't bark," said a soldier. "Dogs bark. We should call it a prairie dog." "That's it!" Lewis and Clark agreed.

Lewis and Clark picked a scout to take the prairie dog to the president. Clark also gave the scout some birds to take. They were called magpies. Lewis gave the scout a letter for the president. He gave him plants that he had collected. The soldiers gave him buffalo skins and deer horns. "Have a nice trip!" said Lewis and Clark.

The scout and the animals rode a barge down the river. They boarded a big ship in New Orleans. The ship sailed around Florida.

Then it sailed north to Baltimore, Maryland.

Finally, the ship landed in Baltimore.

The scout put the animals and the other presents into the back of a wagon. He paid the driver to take everything to President Jefferson in Washington, D.C.

The president met the wagon at the White House. He picked up the prairie dog's cage. "Is this a gopher?" he asked. "No," said the driver. "I think it is a woodchuck." President Jefferson read the letter from Lewis. "A soldier named this creature a prairie dog. It lives on the Western prairie and barks like a dog."

The president gave the prairie dog a piece of apple. *Chomp!* The prairie dog gobbled it right up. The president laughed. "Americans will want to see this little fellow," he said. "I will send these fine presents to Mr. Peale's museum."

Think Aloud

[2]This part was mostly about how Lewis and Clark and their helpers began their exploration of the West. They were trying to find a new animal they could send back to President Jefferson. They just saw a prairie dog. I wonder how they'll catch it.

Genre Study

Nonfiction/ Expository: The characters in this nonfiction/expository selection are based on real people. But the words they speak in the story may not be the exact words the real people spoke long ago.

Mr. Peale's museum was in Philadelphia. The prairie dog and the other gifts rode in a stagecoach to the museum. It was a very bumpy ride.

Mr. Peale loved the presents. He sent President Jefferson a thank-you note. "The prairie dog is a pleasing little animal. He is not at all dangerous like a groundhog," he wrote.

Mr. Peale put the cage in a sunny room.

Children came to see the prairie dog. Artists came to draw its picture. The visitors touched the buffalo skins and the deer horns. They stared at the magpies. "The American West must be a wonderful place," they said.

The West *was* wonderful. Lewis and Clark were gone for two years exploring it. In November of 1805, they finally reached the Pacific Ocean.[3] They were heroes.

If you travel west today, you can still see some of the sights Lewis and Clark saw. You can see grizzly bears and buffalo. You can see jackrabbits and magpies. And if you are lucky, you might even see a prairie dog!

Think Aloud

[3] *Wow! It took two years for Lewis and Clark to explore the West. They must have had many adventures. I wonder how they felt when they reached the Pacific Ocean. I would like to find out more about their adventures.*

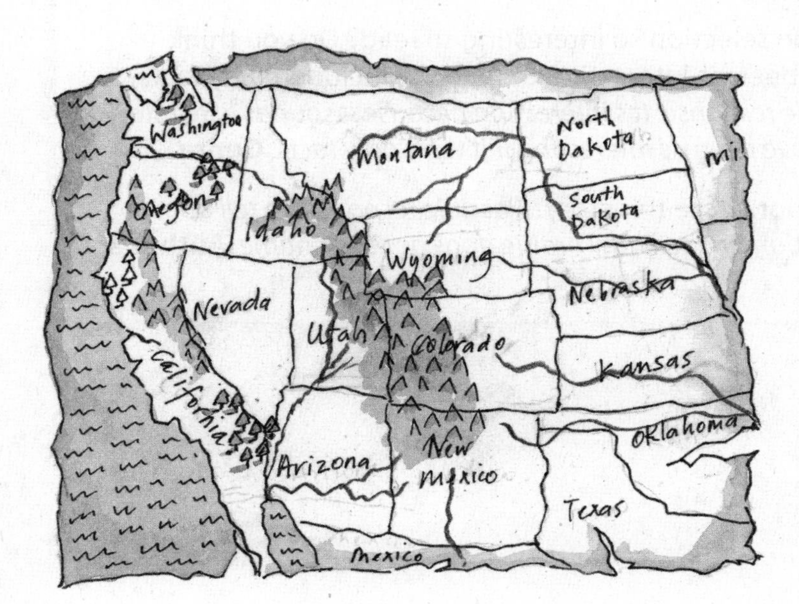

After Reading

Retell: Have children list one or two facts that they learned about Lewis and Clark while listening to the selection.

Student Think Aloud

"I figured out _____ because . . ."

Use Copying Master number 4 to prompt children to share something that they figured out while listening to the story.

Cultural Perspective

Sacagawea was from the Shoshone tribe. Her name means "bird woman." She was a very helpful member of the team because she could talk to Shoshone Indians they met along the way. She also remembered trails through the West that she had used during her childhood. She was the only woman on the expedition.

Think and Respond

1. Why did the president want Lewis and Clark to send presents? *Possible response: so he and other people could see what the West was like.* **Inferential**
2. What makes this nonfiction selection so interesting to read? Do you think the selection would have been as interesting to read if it included only facts? *Responses will vary. Possible response: It's interesting because it sounds like a story. No, I don't think it would have been as interesting if it were only facts.* **Genre**
3. Why do you think the author wrote this story? *Possible response: to tell about the Lewis and Clark expedition and tell how prairie dogs got their name* **Author's Purpose**

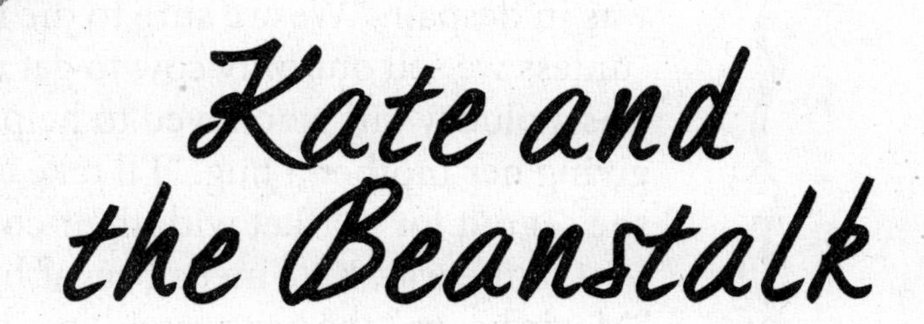

Kate and the Beanstalk

a fairy tale
by Mary Pope Osborne

Genre: Fairy Tale
Comprehension Strategy: Summarize
Think-Aloud Copying Master number 7

Before Reading

Genre: Tell children that a fairy tale is a story about both good and bad make-believe characters such as talking animals, fairies, elves, or giants. Invite children to recall any fairy tales they may have heard or read before, such as "Jack and the Beanstalk" or "The Ugly Duckling."

Expand Vocabulary: Introduce these words before reading:

humble: modest, simple

forlorn: sad

giantess: a female giant

avenge: punish somebody for a wrong done

Set a Purpose for Reading: Have children listen to find out what happens to Kate when she climbs the beanstalk.

During Reading

Use the Think Alouds during the first reading of the story. The genre note may be used during subsequent readings.

Kate and the Beanstalk

by Mary Pope Osborne

Long ago, a girl named Kate lived with her mother in a humble cottage. One day, after a hard winter, Kate's mother was in despair. "We are sure to die from hunger," she said, "unless we sell our only cow to get money for food." Kate was a plucky girl who loved to help. "Don't worry," she said, giving her mother a hug. "I'll take care of everything." And she set out for market with their cow.

On the way, Kate met a beggar holding a small sack. "Magic beans," the beggar said in a creaky voice. "How extraordinary!" said Kate when she saw them, for the brown beans shone like dark gold. "I don't think I can live without them." "They can be yours—in exchange for your cow," said the beggar. Without another thought, Kate traded her cow for the beans and rushed home to give them to her mother.[1]

But to Kate's surprise, her poor mother was horrified. "Our only hope is gone!" she cried. "Now we will surely starve!" And she tossed the beans out the window. Hungry and forlorn, Kate went to bed.

During the night, Kate couldn't sleep. She got up and crept into the moonlit garden. She gasped. For in the darkest corner, a giant beanstalk rose into the sky. It rose higher and higher and higher still, till it disappeared behind the clouds. "Does it never end?" whispered Kate. Without waiting for morning, Kate began climbing the beanstalk. She climbed and climbed and climbed . . .

. . . up and up and up.

When Kate reached the top, light was creeping into the gray sky. Through a misty haze, she saw the most astonishing sight: Above the clouds was a countryside with fine woods, a crystal stream, a rolling sheep meadow, and a mighty castle. As Kate stared in wonder, an old woman hobbled out of the woods. "Hello!" said Kate. "Is that castle your home?"

"No, my dear," the woman replied. "It once belonged to a noble knight and his fair wife. They had a small infant and many treasures. But one day, a monstrous giant came to steal from them. He killed the good man and took over his castle." "How dreadful!" said Kate. "Fortunately, the

Think Aloud

[1]*This was mostly about how a poor girl takes her cow to market to sell, and trades it for some beans. This reminds me of another fairy tale that I have read called "Jack and the Beanstalk." Up to this point both are poor, and sell their cow for a bag of beans.*

knight's wife and baby were visiting in the valley," said the old woman. "Afraid to return home, the grieving widow stayed below to raise her child. But alas, now they are very poor and close to starving." "That's so sad," said Kate. "Sadder than you know, my dear," replied the old woman. She looked deeply into Kate's eyes. "Perhaps you are the one to right the terrible wrongs that have occurred." "Me?" said Kate.

"Are you afraid?"

"I don't think so. I fear nothing when I'm doing right. How can I help?" said Kate.

"The knight had three precious treasures—a hen that lays golden eggs, a bag filled with gold coins, and the most wondrous harp in all the world," said the old woman. "If you find these and return them to the knight's widow, then she and her child will not die from hunger." Kate took a deep breath. "I shall try," she said. Kate bid farewell to the old woman, then strode across the sheep meadow. As she approached the castle, a giantess lunged into the early morning light.

"Help me!" the huge woman roared. "My husband makes me cook from the cock's crow to the owl's hoot! Whenever I hire servants, he gobbles them up!" "I'll be your servant," said Kate. "But you must hide me from the giant." Kate helped the giantess make breakfast until the sun came up. When she heard the giant coming down the hall, she trembled with fear. His footsteps sounded like the booms of a cannon. "Hide!" whispered the giantess, and she pushed Kate into a closet.[2]

Peeking through the keyhole, Kate watched and listened. "Fee, Fi, Fo, Fum'un, I smell the blood of an Englishwoman. Be she alive or be she dead, I'll grind her bones to make my bread."

"Don't be silly," said the giantess. "You only smell the wagonload of bacon I fried for your breakfast." "Oh," said the giant.

When the giant finished eating, he said, "Bring me the knight's hen." The giantess brought out a small brown hen. "Lay!" ordered the giant. And the little hen laid a golden egg. "Ha-ha-haah!" roared the giant. "I love my lovely little stolen hen." Then he put down his head and fell asleep, snoring as loud as thunder. Ever so quietly, Kate crept out of the closet.

She grabbed the hen and rushed from the castle. She ran across the sheep meadow to the beanstalk. Down and down and down she climbed and climbed and climbed, until she

Genre Study

Fairy Tale: Fairy tales contain magical or make-believe objects and people that are not found in real life. This fairy tale includes magic beans, a magic hen, a singing harp, and giants.

Think Aloud

[2] At first I thought the giantess would hurt Kate. But then I found out that the giantess needs Kate's help. I hope Kate can stay hidden from the giantess's husband.

landed *kerplop* in the garden. Kate sighed with relief. "It's better if Mother doesn't know of the danger I've been in," she whispered to the hen. "Stay here, until I can return you to the knight's poor widow." Kate hid the hen behind a bush, then slipped back inside her house.

Kate knew she must disguise herself to return to the castle. That night she dressed in a wig and a beard, crept out to the moonlit garden, and climbed the beanstalk again. Kate climbed and climbed and climbed . . .

. . . up and up and up.

In the light before dawn, Kate crossed the sheep meadow and knocked on the castle door. When the giantess came out, she roared, "Help me! I need a servant! The last one stole our hen and ran way!"

All happened as before. Kate helped the giantess make breakfast until the sun came up. When they heard the giant's booming footsteps and bellowing voice, the giantess hid Kate in the closet. "Fee, Fi, Fo, Fum'un, I smell the blood of an Englishwoman. Be she alive or be she dead, I'll grind her bones to make my bread."

"Calm down," said the giantess. "You only smell the mountain of hash I made for your breakfast." "Oh," said the giant. When the giant finished eating, he said, "Bring me the knight's money bag." The giantess brought out a bag filled with gold coins and the giant greedily counted them.

"Ha-ha-haah!" he roared. "I love my lovely little stolen coins." Soon the giant's head began to nod. Kate watched him fall asleep. Then she crept out and grabbed the money bag. She ran out of the castle and across the sheep meadow to the beanstalk.

Down and down and down . . .

. . . she climbed and climbed and climbed, until she landed *kerplop* in the garden. "Goodness!" said Kate. "What a day! I must hide these coins until I can return them to the knight's poor widow." Kate hid the money bag with the hen, then slipped back inside her house.

That night, Kate disguised herself once again and started up the beanstalk. She climbed and climbed and climbed . . .

. . . up and up and up.

She ran across the sheep meadow, and just as the sun came up, she knocked on the castle door. When the giantess

came out, she grabbed Kate and cried, "Help me! I need a servant! The last one stole our money bag and ran away!"

Again, all happened as before. Kate helped the giantess make breakfast. Soon the giant's footsteps boomed down the hall, and the giantess hid Kate in the closet. "Fee, Fi, Fo, Fum'un, I smell the blood of an Englishwoman. Be she alive or be she dead, I'll grind her bones to make my bread."

"You old fool," said the giantess. "You only smell the sea of fish soup I made for your breakfast." "Oh," said the giant. When the giant finished his soup, he cried, "Bring me the knight's singing harp."

The giantess brought out a magnificent harp, the only one of its kind in the world. The harp sparkled with diamonds and rubies, and it had strings made of gold. "Sing!" bellowed the giant. The harp began to sing a sad, haunting song. It sang of the past, of the noble knight, his lost wife and child, of golden days and starry nights. The harp's lovely song nearly broke Kate's heart. When the giant fell asleep, she crept out from behind the door, seized the harp, and ran away with it.

But the harp was so frightened, it sang high, fearful notes: "*Help me! Help me! Help me!*" "Quiet!" said Kate. "I'm going to return you to the knight's poor widow!" But the giant had already been awakened. He jumped up and with a shout, he ran after Kate.

Kate flew like the wind across the sheep meadow. She grabbed the beanstalk and started down with the harp, the giant fast on her heels.

Down and down and down . . .

. . . she climbed and climbed and climbed, and the giant climbed and climbed and climbed right after her. As soon as Kate's feet touched the ground, she shouted, "Mother! Bring the ax! Hurry!" Kate's mother ran out with the ax, and Kate grabbed it.

"Stand back, Mother!" Kate cried. With one mighty blow, Kate chopped the beanstalk in two. Down and down it fell, down through the sky, and down fell the giant—*WHUMP!*—down into the garden, breaking his neck. The ground shook like an earthquake. Kate's mother took one look and cried out in horror, "That's the giant that killed your father!" "My father?" asked Kate.

Think Aloud

[3]Oh! I figured out that Kate's father was the knight. So that means that Kate and her family used to live in the castle before the giant stole it.

Before her mother could answer, a fairy approached in a chariot drawn by two peacocks. "Greetings, brave Kate," she said. "As Queen of the Fairies, I have long wanted to avenge the treachery done to the good knight. But first I needed to know if his daughter was worthy of her inheritance. So I disguised myself as both the beggar and the old woman and sent you on your quest to your father's castle."[3] "My father's castle?" Kate looked at her mother, who nodded. "I never spoke of your father after he was slain," Kate's mother said. "He would be most proud of you now."

Kate hugged her mother, and they wept for the sorrow and wonder of it all. Then they climbed into the chariot and rose through the clouds, to the castle that was once again theirs . . .

. . . up and up and up.

Kate asked the giantess to stay on as their cook. "Thank you for your kindness," said the giantess. "Would you like a biscuit and jam?" "Indeed," said Kate and her mother. And the giantess served them a biscuit as big as a cow.

After Reading

Retell the Story: Have children act out the story. Assign the roles of Kate, the mother, beggar, old woman, giant, giantess, and fairy queen.

Student Think Aloud

Use Copying Master number 7 to prompt children to summarize the beginning, middle, and end of the story.

"This was mostly about . . ."

Think and Respond

1. What does this story tell you about the kind of person Kate is? Would you climb up the beanstalk if you were Kate? Why or why not? *Possible response: Kate is very brave and honest. Yes, I would climb up the beanstalk because I would be curious.* **Critical**

2. What parts of the story tell you that this is a fairy tale? *Possible responses: the giant and giantess, the hen that lays golden eggs, the fairy, the magic beans* **Genre**

3. Why do you think the author wrote this fairy tale? *Possible response: to entertain listeners with a story filled with adventure and magic* **Author's Purpose**

A Dress for the Moon

a story

by Indira Krishnan

Genre: Fiction Narrative
Comprehension Strategy: Generate Questions
Think-Aloud Copying Master number 1

Before Reading

Genre: Tell children that a narrative is a story that has characters and a setting where the story takes place, and tells about a fictional event. The characters in this story are a man, a coconut tree, and the moon. Remind children of other narratives they have enjoyed hearing, such as "Barnyard Lullaby" and "A Special Trade."

Expand Vocabulary: Introduce the following words before reading:

boastful: bragging about special talents or skills

handiwork: work done by hand

resolved: decided

vain: extremely proud of oneself

Set a Purpose for Reading: Have children listen to find out what happens when Madan tries to make a dress for the moon.

During Reading

Use the Think Alouds during the first reading of the story. Notes about the genre and cultural perspective may be used during subsequent readings.

A Dress for the Moon

by Indira Krishnan

Once upon a time a young man named Madan lived in a village in northern India. Madan's father wanted him to become a farmer. But Madan wished to leave the village and find work in town. He promised his father that he would send a part of his earnings home regularly. His father blessed him and wished him a safe trip.

In town, Madan learned to be a tailor. He worked hard and soon became known for the fine clothes he made. The entire town wanted clothes sewed by Madan. The more his fame spread, the more proud and boastful Madan became.

One night Madan sat gazing at the full *moon* that shone from behind a tall coconut tree. He said, "I am sure I can make a *dress* for the *moon*. The *moon* will praise my handiwork, and then my fame will spread to the sun and stars."

A breeze carried his words to the coconut tree. Laughing softly, the tree bent down and whispered, "That's one thing you can't do."

Madan frowned. "How do you know what I can do?" he said. "You are only a tree."

The coconut tree tried to say something more, but Madan would not listen.

"If you want to be of some use, tell the *moon* that I want to make a *dress* for her. You are tall enough to do that," he said.[1]

So the tree told the *moon* about Madan. The *moon* agreed to have a *dress* made by the famous tailor from Earth.

Madan jumped for joy. Quickly he began to sew a *dress* of smooth white satin for the *moon*. When it was done, he called out to the coconut tree, "You must give this *dress* to the *moon*, as I cannot reach her." The coconut tree agreed.

The following evening, as Madan waited eagerly for the *moon* to appear, the coconut tree bent down and whispered, "The *moon* says your *dress* doesn't fit. It's too loose."

Madan was stunned. "It can't be!" he cried. "The clothes I make always fit perfectly." But the *moon* returned the *dress* to him, and he had to redo it. He spent the night making the *dress* a little smaller and gave it back to the tree.

Genre Study

Narrative: Most fictional narratives are written in the third person. The story is told by a narrator and uses the words *he, she,* and *they.*

Think Aloud

[1]*Madan became proud. He thinks he can make a dress for the moon. The moon is really very far away and big. I wonder how he will make a dress for it?*

The next evening the *moon* rose a little later. Madan waited impatiently. But again the coconut tree bent down and whispered, "The *dress* is still too loose."[2]

Madan nearly wept with disappointment. "I can't believe it! How could I go wrong?" he wailed.

"I tried to tell you before," said the tree. "After the *moon* is full, she grows smaller each day until you can't see her at all. I have been noticing this for many years. So how can you make one *dress* that would fit the *moon* properly? But you wouldn't listen to me."[3]

Brokenhearted, Madan sat with his head in his hands the whole night.

At the break of day he saw the *moon* on the other side of the sky. He whispered, "I am sorry, dear *Moon*. I am not as great a tailor as I thought."

"It's all right," said the *moon*. "After all, I'm the *moon*. How can I wear clothes as people do?"

From that day on, Madan resolved to work harder than before. He was not vain anymore, and his hard work brought him more money. He remembered to send a good part of it to his father. People liked him better because he was an excellent tailor and a humble one, too.[4]

Think Aloud

[2] *It's funny that the greatest tailor on Earth is getting the moon's size wrong. I wonder why?*

Think Aloud

[3] *I thought the coconut tree was an important character in this story because it is so wise. The tree knew all along that the moon changes shape. Madan should have listened to the tree the first time it tried to tell him this. Maybe Madan will be nicer now.*

Think Aloud

[4] *I was right. Madan is much nicer now. I think he learned a lesson about pride and boasting from his experience with the moon's dress.*

After Reading

Retell the Story: Have children summarize what happened at the beginning, middle, and end of the story.

Student Think Aloud

Use Copying Master number 1 to prompt children to share which parts of the story they wondered about.

Think and Respond

1. Would the dress have fit the moon if it tried it on another day? *Possible response: Yes, the dress would have fit when the moon was full again.* **Analytical**

2. What parts of this narrative are make-believe? What parts could really have happened? *Possible responses: The talking tree and moon are make-believe; the boastful tailor and his father could be real people.* **Genre**

3. What might the author want you to learn about the dangers of boasting and having too much pride? *Possible responses: You shouldn't boast too much about your talents. You are not kind to others when you have too much pride.* **Author's Purpose**

When Elephant Goes to a Party

a story

by Sonia Levitin

Genre: Fiction Narrative

Comprehension Strategy: Analyze Story Structure

Think-Aloud Copying Master number 4

Before Reading

Genre: Remind children that a fiction narrative is a made-up story. Ask children to recall other narratives they have heard, such as "A Dress for the Moon."

Expand Vocabulary: Introduce the following words and phrases before reading:

prepared: ready and able to do something

mumble: speak quietly and unclearly

drapes: long curtains

ask permission: ask the host or hostess to let you do something

call collect: make a long-distance telephone call where the person being called agrees to pay the fee

Set a Purpose for Reading: Have children listen to find out what Elephant should do when she goes to a party.

During Reading

Use the Think Alouds during the first reading of the story. Notes about the genre and cultural perspective may be used during subsequent readings.

When Elephant Goes to a Party

by Sonia Levitin

When you take Elephant to a party, it helps to be prepared. First ask if you may bring a guest.

The host or hostess will smile and say politely, "Of course. Any friend of yours is a friend of mine."

Elephant will wonder what to wear. Should she dress up? Or will everyone be wearing jeans? For a swim party, Elephant will need to take a bathing suit. For dancing, she might want ballet shoes. Elephant will enjoy the party more if she is wearing the right clothes for the occasion.[1]

If it's a birthday party, Elephant should take a gift. Help Elephant decide what the birthday person might like. If you don't know, take something that Elephant likes. That means peanuts.

Even if it's not a birthday party, Elephant could take a little present, like flowers or candy. This is a nice way of saying, "Thank you for inviting me."

Before the party, Elephant should take a bath or shower. She should trim her toenails and brush her teeth and tusks. She might want you to tie a ribbon on the end of her tail or braid some flowers into her hair.

At the party, be sure to introduce Elephant to everyone you know. Stay close to her and say, "This is my friend, Elephant." Then tell something pleasant about her. "She is very good at carrying trunks." Elephant should smile and say, "Hello." She should say something friendly, like "What a lovely hat! Where did you get it?" But she must never ask the price. That would be rude.

Elephant should make sure to greet all the grownups, too. "Hello, my name is Elephant. What's yours?"

When they speak to her, Elephant should stand still without jumping or scratching or thumping. Elephant should answer questions nicely and not mumble. She should keep her foot and her tail out of her mouth. Most elephants can sit down gently so the chair won't fall apart.

Elephant should not climb on the furniture or swing on the drapes. She should not turn on anything that is off or turn off anything that is on.

Genre Study

Fiction Narrative: This narrative is written in third person. The narrator tells what Elephant should and should not do and uses the word *she*.

Think Aloud

[1]*I figured out this story is fiction because elephants don't really dress up in clothes and go to birthday parties.*

Elephant should not touch things that might break. If Elephant happens to break or spill something, she should quickly apologize and help clean up the mess.

If Elephant wants something, she should ask first, "May I?" She should wait until food is offered. That means candy, too.

Then Elephant should take only a few, and not fill her trunk with goodies to take home.

If there are pets in the house, Elephant must leave them alone, unless they ask to play with her first. Strange monkeys, cats, and alligators should be left in peace.

There might be toys for everyone to share or games like Pin the Tail on the Donkey or Musical Chairs. Sometimes there are prizes for everyone. Elephant should say "Thank you" for the prize. She will take only her own prize home.

When it's time for games, Elephant must line up with the other guests to take her turn. If she pokes somebody by mistake, Elephant should say, "Excuse me." Elephants mustn't push.

If Elephant has to go to the bathroom, what might she do? She should whisper to you and you will whisper, too, and find out where the bathroom is and take her, quick! Before Elephant joins the party again, she should wash with soap and water. She need not take a bath at the party.

Tell Elephant not to snoop. She should stay out of closets and cupboards and secret places. Guests must mind their own business, or they could be in for unpleasant surprises.[2]

If Elephant needs to use the telephone, she should ask permission. She should not talk too long. If she is calling relatives in Arabia or Africa, she should definitely call collect.

When the cake and ice cream come, Elephant may have some, but not all of it. She should not eat the flowers or the paper plates.

Elephant should use her napkin to wipe her mouth.

She should not sit on the cake or toss her spoon across the table.

Elephant must not blow out the birthday candles; that is for the birthday person to do.

If Elephant brought a present to the party, she should not wave her trunk and screech, "Open mine first!"

She should watch and wait.

Soon the birthday person will open Elephant's present and show it to everyone and say, "Wow! This is just what I wanted. Thank you, Elephant."

Think Aloud

[2] *I wonder what* snoop *means. The narrator says that Elephant should stay out of secret places and mind her own business. So I think* snoop *means to go places you shouldn't, such as in bedrooms and closets. These are private places that the host or hostess might not want other people to see.*

Elephant should say, "You're welcome." Elephant cannot take the birthday present home again. It belongs to the birthday person.

Before leaving, Elephant should thank the party giver. She should never leave the party before saying good-bye.[3] And she shouldn't cry. Elephant tears are slippery on the floor.

Elephant will tell the party giver, "I had a very good time. Thank you for inviting me."

The host or hostess will reply, "It was a pleasure having you. Thank you for coming."

The birthday person will say, "Thank you for the present." Elephant will blow a kiss.

You will probably both be invited to many more parties after this.

Think Aloud

[3] I can see what this story is mostly about. Even though the main character is an elephant, it's not about elephants. This story is mostly about good party manners. Even though the story is made-up, the facts about good manners can be used in real life.

Retell the Story: Have children draw three pictures to show three of the party rules the story told about. Have them use their pictures to retell the story.

Student Think Aloud

Use Copying Master number 4 to prompt children to share what they figured out about the story.

"I figured out _____ because . . ."

Cultural Perspective

The narrator states that Elephant might call relatives in Arabia or Africa. In real life, there are two types of elephants: African and Indian. African elephants live in Africa. Indian elephants live in India and Southeast Asia.

Think and Respond

1. What might happen if Elephant does not use good party manners? *Possible response: She would not be invited to other parties.* **Analytical**
2. Which parts of this story are realistic? Which parts are make-believe? *Possible responses: The rules for good manners are realistic; the idea of elephants going to parties is make-believe.* **Genre**
3. Why do you think the author wrote this story? *Possible response: She wants you to learn good manners in a fun way.* **Author's Purpose**

If You Were a Writer

a story

by Joan Lowery Nixon

Genre: Fiction Narrative
Comprehension Strategy: Generate Questions
Think-Aloud Copying Master number 1

Before Reading

Genre: Remind children that a fiction narrative has made-up characters and events. In this particular selection, the characters and events are realistic but they have been made up by the author. Invite children to think of other fiction narratives they have heard, such as "A Dress for the Moon."

Expand Vocabulary: Introduce the following words before reading:

spell: a curse or hex

dashed: ran, hurried

imaginary: make-believe, fantasy

shiver: shake, tremble

Set a Purpose for Reading: Have children listen to find out how a writer works.

During Reading

Use the Think Alouds during the first reading of the story. The genre note may be used during subsequent readings.

If You Were a Writer

by Joan Lowery Nixon

"*If you were a writer,* you would think of words that make pictures."

Melia's mother was a writer. Sometimes she sat at her computer and her fingers bounced over the keys. Sometimes she stared at the page in the computer and sat so still that Melia thought she was like a fairy-tale princess who had been turned into stone by an evil spell.

"I would like to be a writer, too," Melia told her mother. "Then I could work with a computer, the way you do."

Mother shook her head. "A writer doesn't work just with a computer. A writer works with words. If you were a writer, you would think of words that make pictures."

Melia stroked the sleeve of her mother's silky blouse, and the words *slippery, slithery,* and *soft* slid into her mind.

Uncle John, with the whiskery mustache, opened the front door and called, "Where is everybody?"

Melia ran to hug him, and the words *bristly* and *bushy* bounced into her thoughts.[1]

"Grandma asked me to deliver an apple pie," he said. "It's still hot from the oven." He put the pie on the kitchen counter.

Melia took a deep breath. The pie's fragrance turned into the words *spicy, sweet,* and *sour.*

"Don't you want just a taste?" Uncle John whispered. "I think we should sample it!" He cut a narrow wedge and put it on a plate. They each took a bite, and Melia thought of *tangy* and *tart.*

Uncle John went to talk to Melia's mother, who was still staring at the page in her computer.

"She's under a spell," Melia told him.

"It's not a bad kind of spell," Mother said. "It's just called 'thinking of what to write next.'"

"When do you get out of the spell?" Melia asked.

"When the right words come," Mother said.

"How do you know what they are?"

"If you were a writer you'd know," Mother said. "You'd feel them inside you, and you'd know they were right."

Melia went outside. She climbed into the branches of the oak tree, and watched afternoon melt into evening, and tried the feel of words. She saw a flash of gold streak through an orange sunset, and she murmured, "*Glittery and glowing.*"

Think Aloud

[1] *I was able to picture in my mind what Melia's Uncle John looks like because the words* whiskery mustache, bristly, *and* bushy *help to describe the way he looks.*

"*If you were a writer* you'd know," Mother said. "You'd feel them inside you, and you'd know they were right."

Soon the early evening stars winked through the deep blue sky and the words she whispered were, "*Sparkling, silvery, shining, and shimmer.*"[2]

And the next day, Melia awoke as the morning exploded into sunlight. She felt warm and cozy as she found the words *bright and brilliant and blazing*, and knew they were the right ones.

At breakfast Melia poured glasses of milk for her little sisters, Nikki and Veronica, and for herself. She took the cereal box away from Nikki, who was still reading the back of it, and dumped some flakes into a bowl.

"Would you like an egg?" Mother asked.

Melia gave the cereal box back to Nikki, who continued to read it. "No, thanks," Melia said. She didn't want to have to think about how to eat eggs. She wanted to think about being a writer instead. "Mom," she asked, "how does a writer tell about what happened in a story?"

Mother took a dirty sock and a tennis shoe from her chair and dropped them on the floor. She sat down and said, "If you were a writer you wouldn't *tell about* what happened in a story. You'd think of words that *show* what is happening. You'd use words that let people see what you see. The characters in your stories wouldn't just walk. They might stomp or stamp."

Nikki looked up and said, "Or stumble or stagger."

"Or tiptoe and trip," Melia suggested.

"Or tumble and twirl," Nikki shouted.

Veronica laughed and bounced in her chair until she spilled her glass of milk.

Mother hurried to find a towel. Melia giggled and said, "And when they were tired they could droop and drop."

"And then what?" Nikki asked.

Melia thought hard until she reached the words that would show what was happening. "Then they could slip between the sheets to snore and sleep!" she said.

After school Melia sat with her mother on the porch swing and watched a large black bee try to squirm inside a quivering honeysuckle blossom.

"Where does a writer get ideas?" Melia asked.

"If you were a writer you would search for ideas," Mother said. "Ideas are everywhere. The more you look for ideas, the more you will find."

"Is the idea the story?"

Genre Study

Fiction Narrative: An author helps readers learn about story characters by describing how they look and act, and by the things they say.

Think Aloud

[2]Melia seems to be good at thinking of describing words. I wonder what else she will need to do to become a writer.

"If you were a writer you would search for ideas."

"No. The idea is just the beginning of the story. If you were a writer you would let ideas bounce in your brain while you watched them grow, and turned them over to see the other sides, and poked them and pushed them and pinched off parts of them, and made them go the way you wanted them to go."

A dog dashed past them, racing down the street. A boy chased the dog, shouting, "Come back! Come back!"

"Maybe the dog and the boy could turn into an idea," Mother said. "Ask yourself, 'What if?'"

"What if what?" Melia wondered.

"What if a diamond necklace has caught on the dog's collar? What if the necklace has been stolen by a pirate? What if the boy is really a detective in disguise? What would happen then?"

Melia thought about the "what ifs."

"I'm going to have a peanut butter and honey sandwich," Mother said. "Would you like one, too?"

"If you were a writer, you'd start your stories with something interesting, so people would want to know what happened next."

Melia followed her mother into the kitchen. Mother poked her head into the kitchen cupboard and said, "That's strange. I just bought a large jar of honey, but I can't find it anywhere."

Melia thought about the missing jar of honey. She asked, "What if we were all in the backyard and a bear squeezed into the house through a front window? What if the bear were under the dining room table, eating the honey, but none of us knew he was there until we sat down at the table for dinner? What would happen then?"

"We'd still need some honey, but we'd have a good idea for a story," Mother answered.

Mother gave Melia half of a peanut butter and strawberry jam sandwich. Melia took a big bite of the sandwich and asked, with her mouth full, "How do you start a story?"

Mother licked jam from her thumb. "If you were a writer you'd start your stories with something interesting, so people would want to know what happened next."[3]

Melia finished her sandwich, wiped her hands on her jeans, and began looking for Veronica. She found her in the bedroom closet, putting her shoes on the wrong feet.

"I'll tell you a story," Melia said.

"Not now," Veronica said. "I want to go outside and play."

"A little black dog dashed down the street and into an alley," Melia said. "He huddled against the wall and whimpered. A monster from outer space was after him and the poor little dog didn't know what to do."

Think Aloud

[3] I notice that even though this story is fiction, there is real information about writing. I wonder if Melia will use all of this information to write a story.

"What dog?" Veronica asked. "What monster? Tell me!"

"Later," Melia said. She looked in the den for Nikki. She was lying on her stomach, putting together a jigsaw puzzle.

"Would you like to hear a story about a bear?" she asked.

"No," Nikki said. "I'm busy."

Melia perched on the arm of the sofa. "A hungry bear came out of a forest and across a clearing to a house. He moved and pushed his way through an open window, and no one who lived in that house knew a dangerous bear was prowling through the kitchen."

Nikki looked up. "A real bear? Whose house? What happened then? Tell me!" "Later," Melia said, "when I know the rest of the story."

The doorbell rang. Melia ran to answer the door. So did her mother. A delivery man stood there. He held a box in his hands. "Sign here," he said. Mother signed, took the box, and thanked him before she shut the door. "My books!" she cried. "They're here! The first copies of my new book!" She sat on the floor in the hallway and tore open the top of the box. She lifted out one of the books and smiled at it and looked through it and hugged it, then handed it to Melia.

Melia liked the picture on the jacket of the book. She liked to see her mother's name on the cover.

"How does an idea turn into a whole story?" she asked.

"If you were a writer, you'd invent an imaginary character who fit into your idea," Mother said.

"Like a boy who helped a little black dog escape from a monster from outer space? Or a girl who saved her family from a bear?" Melia asked.

"Exactly. You'd give this person a problem to solve and maybe friends to help solve it. You'd think of exciting, or funny, or even scary things that would happen to the person in your story.

"If you were a writer, while you ate your cereal, and walked to school, and kicked at leaves, and jumped in puddles, and flopped on the grass, and lay in bed at night waiting for sleep, you would let the story mix and grow with the words in your mind. Together they'd zing and zap and explode into sentences you'd taste and feel and hear. Then you'd know it was time to write down the story so it would never be lost.

"If you were a writer, the stories you wrote might make people laugh, or shiver, or even cry. They'd be your stories. They'd belong to you because they'd be a part of you."[4]

Think Aloud

[4]I thought the words the characters say were important in this story because they told about becoming a writer. Whenever Mother spoke to Melia, she gave her really useful information.

"If you were a writer,
the stories you wrote might make people laugh, or shiver, or even cry."

"And I could decide what to do with them," Melia said.

"That's right," Mother said. "You could hug them to yourself like a warm secret, or you could share them with the whole world . . . if you were a writer."

Mother pulled a small pad of paper and a pencil out of her shirt pocket. At the top of the first page she printed a story, by Melia. She smiled and gave the pad and pencil to Melia. "I think you *are* a writer," she said.

Melia crawled over the box of books to hug her mother. "Oh, yes!" she answered. "I am!"

"If you were a writer,

After Reading

Retell the Story: Have children write a list of the things that Melia's mom says that writers do. Have children use their lists to retell the story.

Student Think Aloud

Use Copying Master number 1 to prompt children to share something they wondered as they listened to the story.

Think and Respond

1. The author explains how story ideas bounce around a writer's head, growing and changing. How can ideas grow and change? Give an example of this from the story. *Responses will vary. Possible response: Ideas grow and change when the writer adds to them to make a story. Melia gets an idea about the boy chasing a dog. She changes this idea into the beginning of a story about a dog that is being chased by an alien.* **Analytical**

2. Even though this is a fictional story, there is information about what a writer does. Name some of that information. *Possible responses: Invent imaginary characters. Let ideas bounce in your head. Start the story with something interesting.* **Genre**

3. Why did the author write this story? *Possible response: She wanted to share information about becoming a writer in an interesting and entertaining way.* **Author's Purpose**

The Bremen Town Musicians

a German folktale

retold by Anne Rockwell

Genre: Folktale

Comprehension Strategy: Generate Questions

Think-Aloud Copying Master number 1

Before Reading

Genre: Remind children that a folktale, such as this one from Germany, is a story that has been told and retold for many years. It often has talking animals. Ask children to recall other folktales that they have heard, such as "Nail Soup."

Expand Vocabulary: Introduce the following words before reading:

gasping: out of breath

lute: a musical instrument similar to the guitar

kettledrum: a large copper or brass drum covered with a parchment skin

suited: to be right for or satisfying to somebody

Set a Purpose for Reading: Have children listen to find out who the Bremen Town Musicians are.

During Reading

Use the Think Alouds during the first reading of the story. Notes about the genre and cultural perspective may be used during subsequent readings.

a German folktale
retold by Anne Rockwell

A man once had a donkey who had carried his wheat to the mill for many a year, but the donkey's strength was going for he was growing old. Then his master began to think about what to do with the old donkey, but the donkey ran away and set out on the road to Bremen.

"There," he thought, "I can surely be town musician."

When the donkey had gone some distance, he came to an old dog, lying in the road, gasping.

"Why are you gasping so, you big fellow?" asked the donkey.

"Ah," said the dog, "because I am old and weak and can no longer hunt, my master wants to kill me. So I ran away as fast as I could, but now, how will I earn my keep?"

"I am going to Bremen," said the donkey. "There I shall be town musician. Come with me, I will play the lute, and you shall beat the kettledrum."

The dog agreed, and on they went.

Before long they came to a cat, sitting in the path, with a face like three rainy days.

"Now, old puss, what has gone askew with you?" asked the donkey.

"Poor me," said the cat. "Because I am now old and my teeth are worn to stumps, I prefer to sit by the fire rather than hunt rats and mice. But my mistress wants to drown me, so I ran away. But where am I to go?"

"Come with us to Bremen," said the donkey. "You understand night music, so you can be a town musician."

The cat thought well of it, and went with them. Then the three passed a farm where a cock was crowing with all his might.

"Your crow goes through my heart," said the donkey. "What is the matter?"

"Oh, I have crowed up the sun for many mornings of many years, but now guests are coming on Sunday, and the cook intends to put me in the soup tomorrow. So I crow while still I can."

"Ah, but Old Red-Comb," said the donkey, "you had better come away with us. We are going to Bremen to be town musicians, and you with your good voice can make fine music with us."[1]

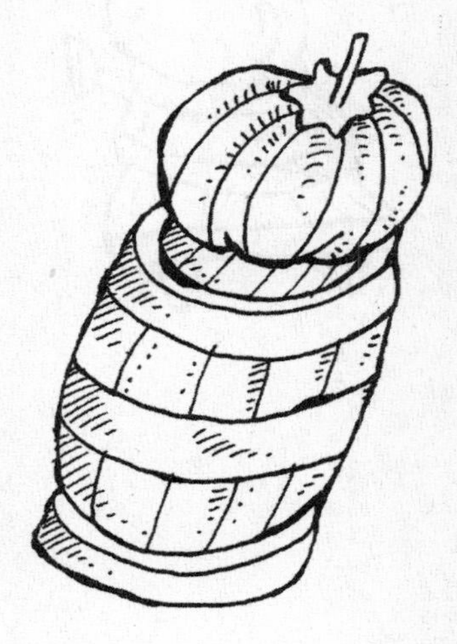

Genre Study

Folktale: Animals in folktales often talk and act just as people do. They also express feelings that people might have.

[1]*Even though the characters in this folktale are animals, they remind me of people because of the way they talk and act.*

The cock agreed and all four went on together. They could not reach Bremen in one day, however, and in the evening they came to a forest. Far off through the trees they saw a little light shining, and they thought there must be a house in the forest.

The dog said, "A few bones with some meat on them would do me good." So they made their way through the forest until they came to a snug little house, which was well lighted. The donkey, being biggest, looked in the window. What did he see but a table covered with good things to eat and drink and four robbers sitting there enjoying themselves. For the musicians had come upon a robber's house.

"If only we were in there!" said the donkey.

So the animals thought of a plan to drive away the robbers. The donkey placed himself with his forefeet upon the windowsill, the dog jumped on the donkey's back, the cat climbed upon the dog, and the cock flew up and perched on the head of the cat.

And then they began to perform their music together. The donkey brayed. The dog barked. The cat meowed, and the cock crowed so loud it broke the window glass.[2] And the robbers jumped up in fright and ran away.

The four musicians sat down at the table and ate and drank all the good things that were left.

As soon as they finished, the four musicians put out the light and found places to sleep. The donkey lay down on some straw in the yard. The dog lay down at the back door. The cat sat by the dying fire, and the cock perched high on a beam of the roof.

When the robbers saw that the light was out in their house and all was quiet, one said, "We shouldn't have been so frightened," and he went back to examine the house.

The robber entered the house and went to light a candle. He mistook the glistening, fiery eyes of the cat for live coals, and held a match to them to light it. But the cat flew in his face, spitting and scratching. The robber was dreadfully frightened and ran to the back door, but the dog jumped up and bit his leg. As soon as he ran across the yard, the donkey gave him a good kick. And the cock began to crow, "Cock-a-doodle-doo!"

The robber ran back into the forest as fast as he could and said to the others, "Oh, there is a horrible witch sitting in our house who spat on me and scratched my face with her long claws. By the back door stands a man with a knife who stabbed

Think Aloud

[2] *At first I thought the animals played their musical instruments. Then I found out that the donkey brayed, the dog barked, the cat meowed, and the cock crowed. I wonder if this will be enough to scare the robbers.*

me in the leg. In the yard there lies a huge monster who beat me with a club, and above the roof there sits the judge who called out, 'Cook him in the stew!' So I got away as well as I could."[3]

After this the robbers never again dared enter the house. But it suited the Bremen town musicians so well that they did not want to leave it. So there they stayed, in comfort and friendship, in the snug little cottage for the rest of their days.

Think Aloud

[3] *I wonder why the robber thought he heard "Cook him in the stew!" Oh yes, that must be how he heard "Cock-a doodle-doo!" They rhyme.*

Retell the Story: Have children act out the story. Assign roles of the animals and robbers.

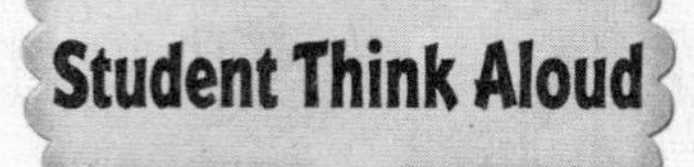

Use Copying Master number 1 to prompt children to share something they wondered about as they listened to the story.

Cultural Perspective
Bremen is a city in Germany. Today in Bremen, there is a famous sculpture of the Bremen Town Musicians.

Think and Respond

1. Did the animals really become the Bremen Town Musicians? Explain. *Possible response: No, because before they even made it to Bremen, they found the cottage that they took over from the robbers.* **Inferential**
2. What parts of this story might have really happened? What parts were make-believe? *Possible response: The owners of the animals might really have mistreated them; the robbers could be real people. The talking animals were make-believe.* **Genre**
3. Why might the author have written this folktale? *Possible responses: to make us laugh; to entertain us with a silly story about talking animals* **Author's Purpose**

So You Want to Be an Inventor?

by Judith St. George

Genre: Nonfiction/Expository
Comprehension Strategy: Generate Questions
Think-Aloud Copying Master number 1

Before Reading

Genre: Remind children that expository text offers information that is true. Invite children to recall other nonfiction selections that they have heard, such as "Police Patrol" and "Lewis and Clark: A Prairie Dog for the President."

Expand Vocabulary: Before reading, introduce these terms:

reaping: cutting and gathering a crop

hoaxer: a trickster or practical joker

torpedoes: weapons that can be fired under water and explode on contact

barriers: obstacles, difficulties

Set a Purpose for Reading: Have children listen to learn about what it takes to be an inventor.

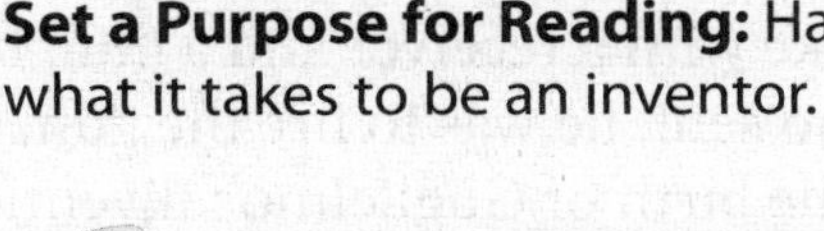

During Reading

Use the Think Alouds during the first reading of the selection. Notes about the genre and cultural perspective may be used during subsequent readings.

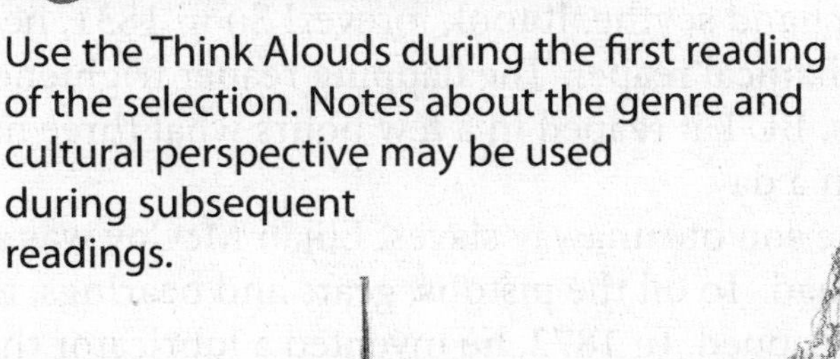

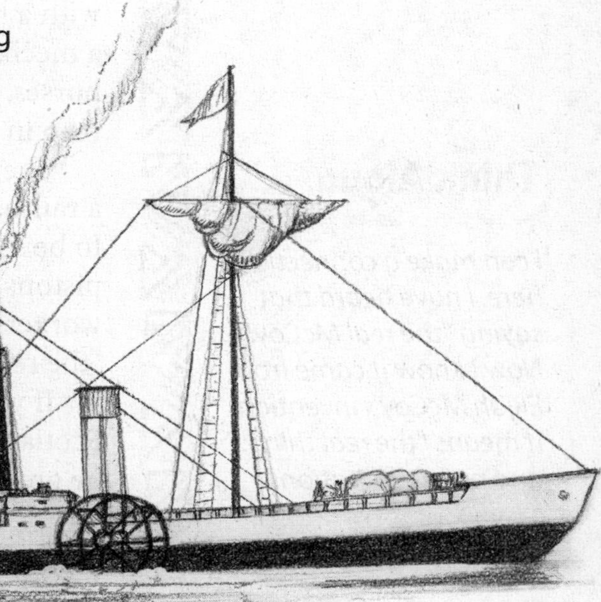

So You Want to Be an Inventor?

by Judith St. George

Are you a kid who likes to tinker with machines that clink and clank, levers that pull, bells that ring, togs that grind, switches that turn on and off, wires that vibrate, dials that spin? You watch TV, ride a bike, phone your friends, pop popcorn in a microwave, go to the movies. Inventions! And you want to be an inventor, too?

You don't have to have white hair and wrinkles to be an inventor. At twelve, Benjamin Franklin invented swim paddles for his hand and kick paddles for his feet. When he grew up, Ben Franklin invented the lightning rod, Franklin stove fireplace damper, library stepstool and odometer to measure the distance that a vehicle travels. At seventy-seven he invented bifocal glasses. (He probably needed them!)

Do you have a brother? Brothers can help! Connecticut patriot David Bushnell would have been sunk without his brother, Ezra. David wasn't strong enough to operate all the cranks, handles and pumps in the submarine he invented during the Revolutionary War, so Ezra did it for him.

In 1895, Guglielmo Marconi had his brother Alfonzo take a mile-and-a-half hike with a receiver and a gun. If he received the signals Guglielmo sent, he was to fire the gun, POW! That gunshot broadcast the birth of Guglielmo's invention—the radio!

If you want to be an inventor, find a need and fill it. Cyrus McCormick got tired of reaping wheat on his family's farm with a hand scythe. It took forever! So in 1831, he invented a mechanical reaper. The flapping reaper frightened the horses. BUT it reaped in a few hours what three men could reap in a day.

The son of runaway slaves, Elijah McCoy was an oilman on a railroad. To oil the pistons, gears and bearings, the train had to be stopped. In 1872, he invented a lubricator that oiled the pistons, gears and bearings while the engine was running! Other workers wanted his invention for their engines. But they wanted "the real McCoy" lubricators—or nothing![1]

If you want to be an inventor, be a dreamer. As a boy in Scotland, Alexander Graham Bell had a "dreaming place." When he grew up, he dreamed of people talking across distances—

Think Aloud

[1] *I can make a connection here. I have heard that saying "the real McCoy." Now I know it came from Elijah McCoy's invention. It means "the real thing, and not an imitation."*

maybe by electric signals. Electric signals it was! In 1876, he invented the telephone!

Young Russian Igor Sikorsky dreamed of a different way to fly—up, down/forward, backward, AND sideways. Igor's brother poked fun at him. "It will never fly!" He was wrong. With its three blades whirling, in 1939 Igor's dream helicopter took off.

If you want to be an inventor, keep your eyes open! On a 1914 trip to Labrador, fur trader Clarence Birdseye watched Eskimos freeze fish on the ice.[2] When the fish thawed, they tasted fresh. Would fast-freezing food between two metal plates work as well? It did! All those frozen dinners, pizzas and other frozen yummies come to you by way of Clarence Birdseye.

After a country walk with his dog in 1948, Swiss engineer Georges de Mestral picked cockleburs off his pants. Why, the cocklebur hooks gripped the wool loops in his pants. Hooks and loops! The perfect fastener! Georges's invention? Velcro!

An inventor has to be as stubborn as a bulldog. Yankee Charles Goodyear spent ten years trying to make raw rubber usable. He spent all his money and was thrown into debtor's jail before he hit the jackpot in 1839 by treating raw rubber with sulphur under heat. Tires, tennis balls, and all sorts of other rubber goodies have been pouncing around ever since!

Think Aloud

[2] I wonder what someone could invent from seeing eskimos freeze fish? I will think about things I know that use freezing. I know! Maybe it was a freezer.

Thomas Edison spent more than a year looking for a thin thread called a filament that would glow without burning up when electricity passed through it. He tried platinum, nickel, gold, silver, fish line, cotton thread, coconut hair, people hair, wood shavings, cork and more. Carbonized bamboo was the answer! Edison's 1879 incandescent lamp (a lamp that stayed lit) brightened lives everywhere.

Don't worry if people laugh at you. Everyone mocked Robert Fulton's steamboat, calling it "Fulton's Folly" and "a floating sawmill caught on fire." But the laughter lost steam in 1807 when Robert's *Clermont* chugged up the Hudson River from New York to Albany with paddle wheels churning and flags waving.

Newspapers laughed at Robert Goddard for trying to invent a space rocket. They called him "Moon Man." And a <u>hoaxer</u>. He was no hoaxer! Thanks to "Moon Man" Robert Goddard's 1926 invention of a liquid-fuel rocket, the spacecraft Apollo 11 landed Americans safely on the moon in 1969.

Inventors aren't all men! Illinois homemaker Josephine Cochran figured other women were as fed up with washing dishes (and red hands) as she was. In 1886, she put together a wooden tub, wire basket and hand pump to invent the very first dishwasher.

Movie star Hedy Lamarr said, "Any girl can look glamorous. All you have to do is stand still and look stupid." Beautiful Hedy Lamarr wasn't stupid! Just before World War II she fled Austria (and Hitler) for the United States, where she and a friend invented a system for guiding torpedoes by radio signals. Her goal? Beat Hitler!

Even Presidents can be inventors. George Washington invented a sixteen-sided treading barn in 1792. Horses trampled over wheat spread on the barn floor. The grain dropped through slots. Eureka! George Washington's wheat supply was dry, stored and ready to be ground into flour.

Thomas Jefferson invented a two-faced clock, one face inside (it told the day, hour, minute—and second) and one face outside (its Chinese gong could be heard three miles away). Jefferson wasn't called smart for nothing. The ropes holding the weights were so long that he cut holes in the floor to let the weights hang in the basement!

Maybe you like to work alone, Alexander Graham Bell worked alone at night, every night, inventing the graphaphone, an iron lung, kites to study flight and, of course, the telephone. "To take night from me is to rob me of life," he declared.

Nikola Tesla was world famous for inventing the alternating-current (AC) motor in the 1880s to produce huge amounts of electricity that could be sent over long distances. But Nikola lived in lonely New York hotel rooms, had no family, few friends, and only worked for himself.

Maybe you'd rather invent as part of a team. Thomas Edison forged a crew of inventors who huddled day and night over clanking, hissing motors, smelly chemicals and machines that sent sparks flying. He—and his crew—came up with the incandescent lamp, the movie camera, the phonograph and more than a thousand other inventions![3]

One invention can lead to another. In the early 1900s, Henry Ford jumped from Michigan Farmboy to King of the Road. He didn't invent the automobile, BUT he did perfect mass production and the moving assembly line that had workers slapping his Model T Ford cars together in a hurry.

Other inventors hopped on board. Mary Anderson invented windshield wipers. (Swish-swish!) Garrett Morgan came up with traffic lights. (Red—stop! Yellow—slow! Green—go!) Elmer

Think Aloud

[3]I noticed the author used examples of famous inventors to give me tips about being an inventor. This makes the information more interesting to learn.

Wavering invented car radios. (A little music, please!) More cars? More accidents? Allen Breed's air bags saved lives. (Whoosh!) Wouldn't Henry Ford be amazed at what he had started!

Sometimes an invention creates more problems than it solves. In 1793, Eli Whitney invented the cotton gin that cleaned cotton fifty times faster than workers cleaning by hand. (Wire spikes pulled cotton through slots too narrow for the seeds.) But more and more slaves were needed to grow more and more cotton. Eli Whitney's cotton gin sowed the seeds of the Civil War!

Watch out! Your invention might scare people. Swedish chemist Alfred Nobel invented dynamite in 1866 by mixing nitroglycerin with chalky soil. But when five workers were killed in an explosion, Alfred was ordered to work outside the city on a barge in the middle of a lake.

While experimenting in 1895, scientist Wilhelm Roentgen was shocked when he turned on an electric switch and saw light rays glowing from a screen he had treated with barium. X rays! People freaked out. Did seeing their own bones mean they would die? Or were X rays really death rays?

Be careful! The truth is, inventing can be dangerous. At an 1854 New York City fair, Elisha Otis stood on a platform that was raised up thirty feet by rope. He ordered the rope cut. The platform fell! But iron teeth grabbed notches in the guide rails and stopped the platform cold. "All safe, gentlemen, all safe!" Elisha called out. His safety brake invention worked!

Some of Orville and Wilbur Wright's early-1900s flying machines landed safely and some didn't. Poor Orville! He was hurt in a glider crash, two airplane crashes and a plane crash that knocked him out and broke his leg and ribs! "Flying machine, cloth, and sticks in a heap, with me in the center," Orville wrote in his diary.

Some inventions are invented before their time.[4] If Leonardo da Vinci hadn't been born more than five hundred and fifty years ago, he could have been one of the greatest! He thought up (and sketched) an air cooling machine, automobile, paddle wheel boat, diver's snorkel, flying machine, parachute and projector for pictures.

In the 1830s, British mathematician Charles Babbage invented a steam-powered "computer" that had a memory bank, made decisions and recorded data. His idea was on target, but his computer had to be trashed for lack of electronic know-how.

Genre Study

Nonfiction/ Expository: The writer uses word choice to make a nonfiction/expository text more fun to read. In this paragraph, she uses onomatopoeia. Onomatopoeia is using words that recreate the sounds they describe, such as the *swish-swish* of windshield wipers.

Think Aloud

[4] *I wonder what the author means when she says that inventors like Leonardo da Vinci invented things "before their time." I think she must mean that they had the ideas for inventions, but the inventions were never really made until much later.*

Keep a sharp eye on your invention—copycats are out there! Joseph Henry invented a telegraph system in the 1830s that sent signals over short distances. In 1844, Samuel F. B. Morse jazzed up Joseph's invention, put together a Morse code dot-dash system, and was tapped as inventor of the telegraph.

In 1847, William Kelly invented a method of producing steel by burning off excess carbon in hot pig iron with a blast of cold air. Eight years later, Henry Bessemer's mammoth, flame-shooting converters produced steel the same way. Who was known as the red-hot steel maker? Henry Bessemer, that's who!

Of course some inventions never take off at all. Andrew Jackson Jr. invented adjustable eyeglasses for chickens so they wouldn't peck each other's eyes out. (The chickens weren't interested.)

John Boax invented a haircutting helmet that sucked hair up into tiny holes where electric coils burned hair to just the right length. (Ouch!)

Elmer Walter invented a table knife with a mirror on the handle to use at meals for checking if food was stuck in his teeth. (Disgusting!)

Franz Vester invented a coffin with an escape hatch and a breathing tube in case the person inside was still alive. (Too gruesome!)

Other inventions take off so well, they're named for their inventor. Electricity is measured in volts (Alessandro Volta invented the electric battery) and watts (James Watt made steam power practical).

Charles Macintosh's weatherproof fabric turned into mackintosh raincoats.

During the French Revolution, Joseph Guillotin's guillotine beheaded victims.

Rudolf Diesel invented the diesel engine that runs on unrefined oil.

Here's the bottom line! Whether your invention is named after you or not, whether you're a dreamer, a loner, are laughed at, work all night or put yourself in danger, your invention could change the world. It has happened!

Vladimir Ziworykin's 1923 electronic tube led to television.

Three U.S. scientists' 1947 transistor led to computers.

Even more important, Johannes Gutenberg invented a hand-operated printing press with movable metal type in the 1440s.

A printer could print in a day what it took a year to write by hand. Result? Books! Books! Books! People decided it was time to learn to read. And they did!

In the end, being an inventor means pushing the limits of what human beings know and what human beings can do. Because you're a risk taker and will be on a quest into the unknown, you have to be willing to try and fail, try and fail, try and MAYBE succeed. One thing is certain: There will always be barriers to be broken, whether it's to find a new source of power, a different way to communicate, a machine that works medical miracles or something that we can't even imagine. It takes passion and heart, but those barriers could be broken by you![5]

Think Aloud

[5]I wonder if I really could become an inventor of something special some day. I know from listening carefully to the selection that no matter what my idea is, I shouldn't give up.

Retell: Have children list three facts they learned from the selection about inventing.

Student Think Aloud

Use Copying Master number 1 to prompt children to share things they wondered about while listening to the selection.

Cultural Perspective

Alfred Nobel, the Swedish inventor of dynamite, created the Nobel Prize. Scientists, inventors, and other world-changing people are honored each year with the prize.

Think and Respond

1. Why does the author say "If you want to be an inventor, be a dreamer"? *Possible response: Inventors need to have good imaginations to think about how they might improve things.* **Analytical**
2. The selection starts by asking the reader questions. Why do you think it starts this way? *Possible response: It helps the reader to make a connection with the inventors and inventions.* **Genre**
3. What character traits does the author want you to know are important for inventors to have? *Possible responses: risk-takers; brave; stubborn; dreamers* **Author's Purpose**

Grandma's Records

a story

by Eric Velasquez

Genre: Fiction Narrative
Comprehension Strategy: Reread
Think-Aloud Copying Master number 7

Before Reading

Genre: Remind children that a narrative is a story that has characters and a setting. Ask children to recall other narratives they have heard, such as "A Special Trade."

Expand Vocabulary: Introduce these terms before reading:

record: a vinyl disc that sound or music is copied onto

percussion: instruments, such as drums and cymbals

subway: an underground railroad

studio: a room where artists work

Set a Purpose for Reading: Have children listen to find out why one record was very special to Grandma.

During Reading

Use the Think Alouds during the first reading of the story. Notes about the genre and cultural perspective may be used during subsequent readings.

Grandma's Records

by Eric Velasquez

Grandma liked all types of music. But one record was very special to her. Whenever she played it, she would put her hand over her heart and close her eyes as she sang along. When it was over, Grandma would sometimes sit quietly, thinking about Grandpa and the old days in Santurce, her hometown.

"Sometimes," Grandma said, "a song can say everything that is in your heart as if it was written just for you."

My favorite days were the ones when Grandma would tell me, "You pick the records today." No matter what I would choose, Grandma would always say, "*Siempre me gusta tú selección.*" (I always like your selection.)

Sometimes I would sneak in Grandma's special song just to watch her put her hand over her heart and sing.

Then she would ask, "*Cómo sabes?*" (How did you know?)

If it was too hot to go outside, I'd spend hours looking through all of Grandma's album covers. I'd pick out my favorites and make sketches of the art. As I drew, I could see the record covers coming to life and the bands performing right there in Grandma's living room.

Grandma never went to any nightclubs to see her favorite bands perform. She was happy just to stay home with me and listen to her scratchy records. But Santurce was home to hundreds of musicians, and she knew a lot of the people who played on the records.

Grandma's nephew Sammy played percussion in Raphael Cortijo's band, the best band in Puerto Rico. One day when the band was in town, Sammy brought over Cortijo and the band's lead singer, Ismael Rivera, for a surprise visit. Home-cooked meals were hard to come by on the road, and they couldn't pass up the chance to taste Grandma's famous *arroz con pollo* (chicken and rice).[1]

After eating dessert, Sammy had another surprise for Grandma: two tickets to the band's first New York concert, and their brand-new record, which wasn't even in the stores yet.

Genre Study

Narrative: This narrative is written in the first person. One of the story characters tells the story from his point of view.

Think Aloud

[1] *Grandma seems like a very nice person. She is close to her grandchild and cooks home meals for her nephew and his band.*

I raced over to the record player, thrilled to be the first New Yorker to hear the latest music.

The theater was all the way up in the Bronx. We took the subway there, and Grandma was nervous during the whole ride.[2] When we got to the theater, we walked past the long line of people and went right inside because of our special tickets. The theater was bigger than all the movie theaters I had ever gone to.

Grandma and I were surprised at how different the music sounded live. The musicians made familiar songs sound fresh by adding new musical phrases and words.

Before the last song began, Ismael said, "This one goes out to Carmen," and he pointed to Grandma as he sang her special song. I looked at her as she put her hand over her heart, raised the other hand, closed her eyes, and began to sing along. Ismael was singing to my Grandma! Then I looked around and realized that everyone in the theater had their hands over their hearts, too.

After the show we went backstage. I asked Ismael how he knew about Grandma's song. He explained that the song was about coming to a new country and having to leave those you love behind. People put their hands over their hearts to show that their hearts remain in Puerto Rico even though they may be far away.[3] Now I understood why Grandma's song was special to so many people.

As I got older, I started bringing over my records to play for Grandma—Brazilian music, jazz, and even rap. She loved listening to it all.

Even now, when I'm playing CDs in my studio, I imagine I'm back in Grandma's living room and she turns to me and says. "You be the DJ today. *Siempre me gusta, tú selección.*" And as I work, Grandma's special song surrounds me.

Think Aloud

[2] I wonder why Grandma is nervous. When I reread, I see the narrator says his grandma never went to nightclubs to hear bands perform live, so I think she is nervous about doing something new.

Think Aloud

[3] I was confused about why the author mentions that Grandma's song was special to so many people. When I reread I see that lots of people put their hands over their hearts, just like Grandma does.

After Reading

Retell the Story: Have children choose a story character and retell the story from his or her point of view.

Student Think Aloud

Use Copying Master number 7 to prompt children to summarize the beginning, middle, and end of the story.

"This was mostly about . . ."

Cultural Perspective

Grandma's special song is a popular Puerto Rican folk song, "In My Old San Juan." San Juan is the capital of Puerto Rico.

Think and Respond

1. What was Grandma's name? How do you know? *Possible responses: Her name was Carmen. I figured this out because Ismael said, "This one goes out to Carmen" as he pointed to Grandma, so her name must be Carmen.* **Inferential**
2. This story is written in first person. Who is telling the story? What do you know about him? *Possible responses: Carmen's grandson is telling the story. He is probably an artist because he talks about working in a studio and he mentions that he used to sketch album covers.* **Genre**
3. What does the author want you to learn about music from this story? *Possible response: Music can bring people together, make them feel good and help them remember happy times.* **Author's Purpose**

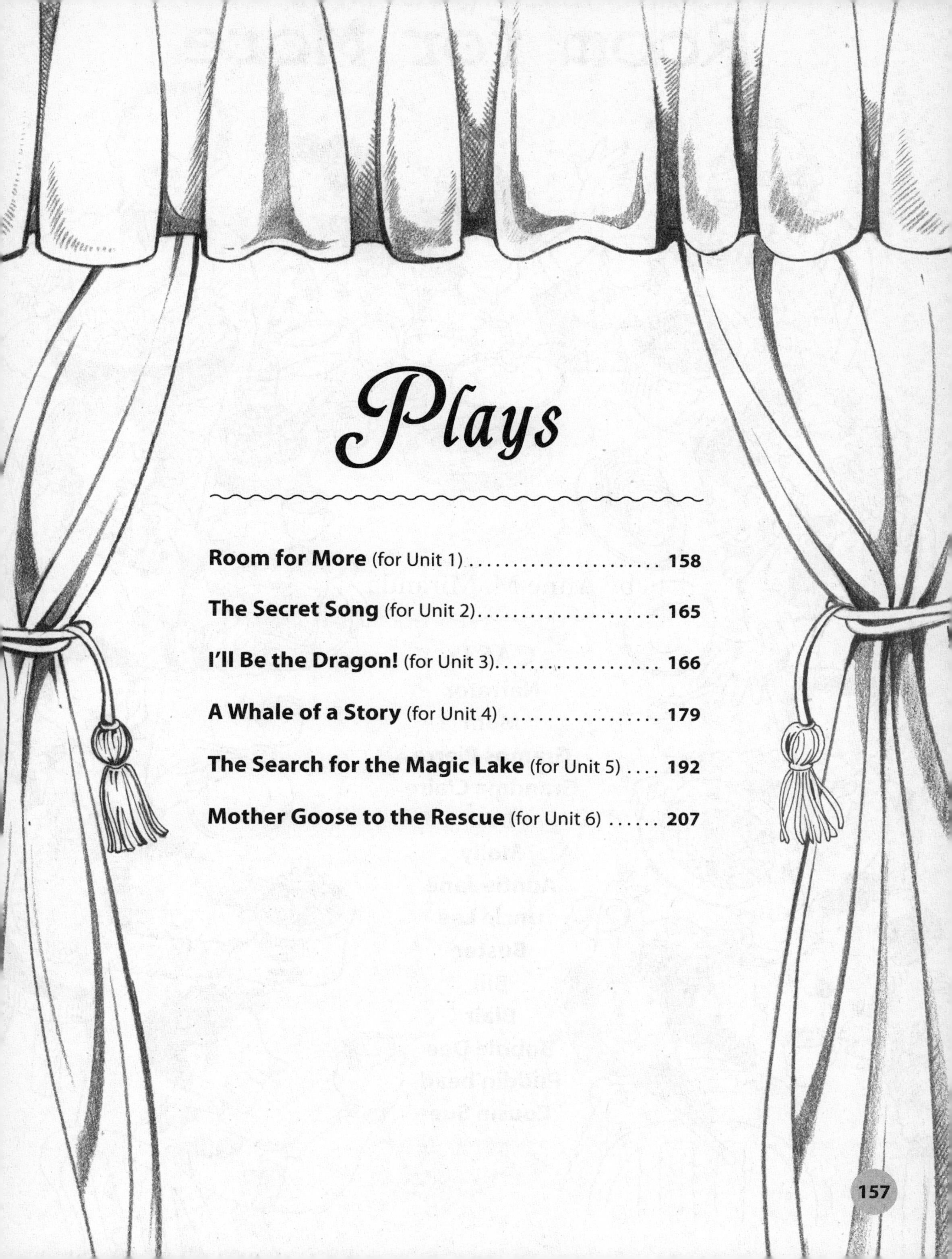

Plays

Room for More

by Anne M. Miranda

CAST:
Narrator
Mom
Gramps Pierre
Grandma Claire
Dad
Molly
Auntie Jane
Uncle Lee
Buster
Bill
Blair
Bobbie Dee
Puddin'head
Cousin Sue

Narrator: Once, not very long ago,
Dad fixed a lunch from Mexico:
refried beans and hot tamales—
a favorite dish of daughter Molly's.
Mother made some mango punch.
Then the three sat down to lunch.
Mom was just about to pour,
when someone knocked on the
front door.

[Knock, knock!]

Mom: Who's there?

Gramps Pierre: It's Gramps Pierre and Grandma Claire.

Grandma Claire: We've just come from the county fair.
We have our little cat, Ling Shoo, and a
pot of Irish stew.

Mom: Molly, would you show them in?

Dad: Sit down and tell us how you've been.

Molly: It's good to see you, Grandma Claire.
It's good to see you, Gramps Pierre.

Dad: Come in, come in, and take a chair.

Narrator: Gramps sat here and Grandma there.
Ling Shoo curled up beneath a chair.
Mom got each a cup and plate.
Then someone slammed the garden gate.

[Knock, knock!]

Mom: Who can it be?

Auntie Jane: It's Auntie Jane and Uncle Lee.
We drove from Knoxville, Tennessee.

Uncle Lee: So glad you're home. We took a chance.
Here's some cheese from Paris, France.

Mom: Molly, would you show them in?

Dad: Sit down and tell us how you've been.

Molly: It's good to see you, Uncle Lee
and Auntie Jane from Tennessee.

Gramps Pierre: Howdy do!

Grandma Claire: How are you?

All: Come in, come in!
Sit down! What's new?

Narrator: Then Uncle Lee gave Mom the cheese,
while Auntie Jane gave Dad a squeeze.
Just then a car pulled in the drive.
They heard more unexpected guests arrive.

[Knock, knock!]

Mom: Who's there?

Buster: Your cousins, Buster, Bill, and Blair.

Bill: And Bart, our dog with shaggy hair.

Blair: Our mother said it would be nice
to bring a dish of Spanish rice.

Mom: Molly, would you show them in?

Dad: Sit down and tell us how you've been.

Molly: It's good to see you, Bill and Blair,
and Buster and Bart with shaggy hair.

Gramps Pierre: Howdy do!

Grandma Claire: How are you?

Auntie Jane: Hello there.

Uncle Lee: Pull up a chair.

All: Come in, come in! There's lots to share!

Narrator: The triplets, Buster, Blair, and Bill,
sat upon the windowsill.
And Bart, the dog with shaggy hair,
flopped in Daddy's favorite chair.
There was hardly room for more,
when someone else knocked on the
door!
[Knock, knock!]

Mom: Who can it be?

Bobbie Dee: It's your nephew, Bobbie Dee.
My ship is in. I'm home from sea.

Puddin'head: And I'm his parrot, Puddin'head.
We've brought some nice Italian bread.

Mom: Molly, would you show them in?

Dad: Sit down and tell us how you've been.

Molly: I'm glad to see you, Bobbie Dee.
Bring Puddin'head and sit by me.

Gramps Pierre: Howdy do!

Grandma Claire: How are you?

Auntie Jane: Hello there.

Uncle Lee: Pull up a chair.

Buster: Oh, my.

Bill: Oh, me.

Blair: Long time, no see.

All: Come in, come in and have some tea.

Narrator: So Grandma Claire, and Gramps Pierre,
and Buster, Bart, and Bill and Blair,
and Auntie Jane and Uncle Lee,
and Mom's young nephew, Bobbie Dee,
gave hugs and kisses all around
until they heard an awful sound.

Puddin'head: SQUEAK-A, CREAK-A, Bobbie boy!
CRICK-A, CROAK-A, ship ahoy!

Narrator: Yes, Puddin'head began to squawk
so loud that no one else could talk.
Bart began to chase Ling Shoo
and Molly wondered what to do.

Molly: There's no more room for us in here.
I wish that I could disappear.

Mom: Let's go outside for some fresh air.

Dad: Go out, go out and take a chair!

Narrator: Mom picked up the cat, Ling Shoo.
Out went Dad and Molly, too.
Grandma Claire and Gramps Pierre,
and Buster, Bart, and Bill and Blair,
and Auntie Jane and Uncle Lee,
and Puddin'head and Bobbie Dee,
all went out for some fresh air.
Each one dragged a folding chair.

Mom: Everybody have a seat.
There's lots and lots of food to eat.

Dad: That's right! Dig in! It sure looks great!
Does anybody need a plate?

Narrator: They tasted food from France and Spain.
Not one relative complained.
As Mom served Grandma's Irish stew,
Molly smiled at what she knew.

Molly: We'll always welcome a new guest.
Unplanned things are often best.

Mom: There's always room for just one more.

[Knock, knock!]

Molly: Oh, boy! There's someone at the door!

Cousin Sue: It's your second cousin, Sue.
I just flew in from Kalamazoo!

Gramps Pierre: Howdy do!

Grandma Claire: How are you?

Auntie Jane: Hello there.

Uncle Lee: Pull up a chair.

Buster: Oh, my.

Bill: Oh, me.

Blair: Long time, no see.

Bobbie Dee: Have some bread.

Puddin'head: My name is Puddin'head.

Molly: Come on out and take a seat.

Cousin Sue: Seeing you is such a treat.

Molly: If someone knocks at our front door—

All: There's always room for just one more!

The Secret Song

by Margaret Wise Brown

Group 1: Who saw the petals drop from the rose?

Group 2: I, said the spider, But nobody knows.

Group 1: Who saw the sunset flash on the bird?

Group 2: I, said the fish, But nobody heard.

Group 1: Who saw the fog come over the sea?

Group 2: I, said the pigeon, Only me.

Group 1: Who saw the first green light of the sun?

Group 2: I, said the night owl, The only one.

Group 1: Who saw the moss creep over the stone?

Group 2: I, said the grey fox, All alone.

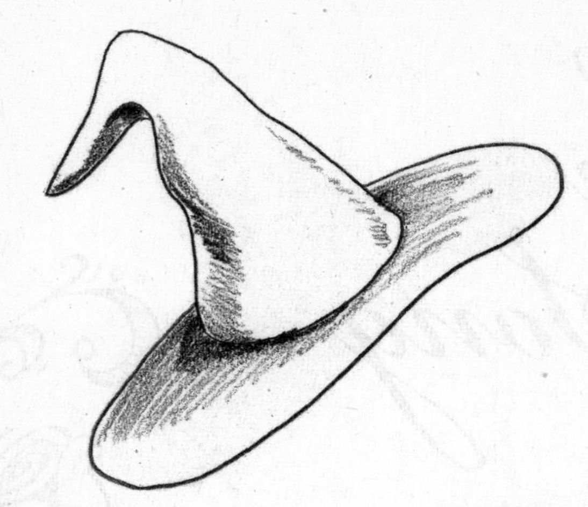

I'll Be the Dragon

by Kathleen M. Fischer

CAST:

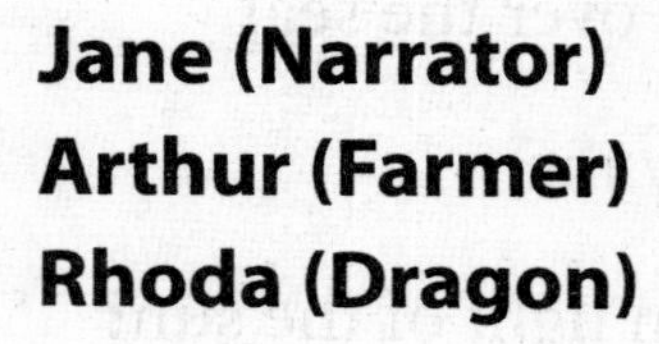

Jane (Narrator)
Arthur (Farmer)
Rhoda (Dragon)

William (Witch)
Sarah (Bird)
Josh (Blacksmith)

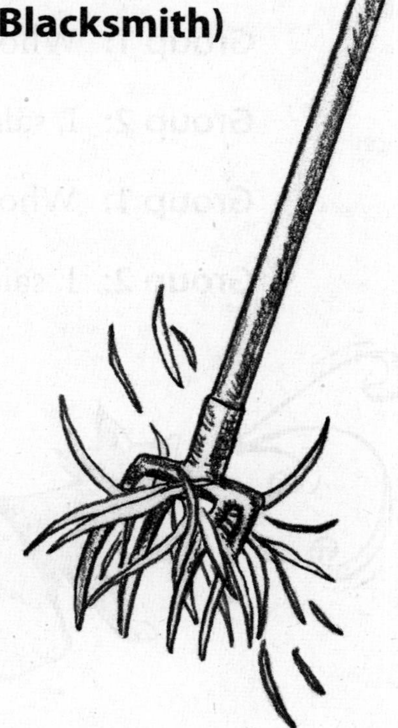

ACT I

Jane: Once upon a time, not so very long ago, some second graders were rehearsing a Readers Theater play.

Arthur: Hey! Have you guys read this play about the dragon? It's going to be great!

Rhoda: You bet! I just love plays about dragons.

William: Yeah! Dragon plays are almost as good as monster plays.

Sarah: Well, if you ask me, the first thing we should do is pick our parts. Has everyone read the play?

All (except Sarah): YES!

Josh: The dragon seems like kind of a sad character. We need someone who can sound sad and not very scary.

William: I can be the dragon. I can really roar. Just listen to this: R-R-R-ROAR!

Arthur: Wait a minute! Dragons don't roar. Besides, this play doesn't have that kind of dragon. He's not a monster. He's sort of nice, really. We need someone who can sound friendly and helpful. Someone like me, for instance.

Sarah: But Arthur, the dragon has to be able to solve people's problems. I'm a great problem solver. I think I should play the dragon.

Josh: Well, everybody knows a dragon should be played by a boy. I'll be the dragon.

Jane: Not so fast! A girl can be a very good dragon. As a matter of fact, I would be perfect!

Rhoda: Listen, I don't want to hurt anyone's feelings, but I was sort of hoping to play the dragon.

William: Hold on! I'm the scariest one here. I still say I should be the dragon.

Jane: Don't get excited. We'll figure this out.

William: How?

Jane: Maybe we should ask Mr. Parks for help.

Sarah: Mr. Parks is busy with another group. Besides, he told us to work this out among ourselves. We haven't given it much of a chance.

Arthur: Well, we can't all be the dragon!

Sarah: Why not? Let's rehearse the play with everyone reading the part of the dragon.

Then nobody will have anything to complain about.

Rhoda: How can we all read the same part? What kind of a play will that be?

Sarah: Let's just try it and see what happens. Everybody look at page one. Ready? Begin!

[long pause]

Arthur: Excuse me, Sarah, but I think we've got a problem. Someone has to read the narrator's part, or we can't even get started.

Jane: Well, I've never been a narrator before, so I'll do it. The rest of you can be the dragon. We'll be fine until we get to page 2.

William: What happens on page 2?

Jane: Look at the dragon's speech in the middle of the page and you'll find out! Go ahead. You read and I'll listen.

All (except Jane): Knock! Knock! Knock! Is anybody home?

[long pause]

Arthur: Oh, I get it! The next line belongs to the witch. If someone doesn't read her part, we won't have a play.

Jane: You got it!

Sarah: What do you think we should do?

Rhoda: Wait a minute! William, tell us again why you wanted to be the dragon.

William: I like sounding scary.

Rhoda: Well, in this play, the scary character is the witch, not the dragon.

William: You're right! I was born to play the witch! The rest of you can be the dragon.

Josh: Now we're getting somewhere.

Sarah: I just read the script again. I think I'd rather have a part all to myself. The bird has some good lines, so I'll be the bird. The rest of you can be the dragon.

Arthur: If Jane and William and Sarah all get their own parts, I want a part of my own, too. I'll be the farmer.

Josh: That means there are only two of us left to read the part of the dragon.

William: Don't forget, we still don't have a blacksmith.

Josh: A blacksmith has to be strong, and we all know I'm the strongest person in this group!

Rhoda: Get real!

William: Give me a break! [together]

Arthur: Sure thing.

Sarah: Come on, Josh.

Josh: Good, I'm glad you agree. I'll be the blacksmith.

Rhoda: And I'll be the dragon!

Sarah: Great. Now, since everybody has a part, let's get to work.

ACT II

Narrator: Once upon a time, long, long ago, there lived a handsome dragon with shiny green scales. You would think that such a magnificent dragon would be happy. But this was not so, for a witch had put a spell on the dragon. And a terrible spell it was, too!

Dragon: Oh, me! Oh, my! Ever since the witch put this spell on me, I can't breathe fire. It really was an accident that my fiery breath burned her brand new broom. Whoever heard of a dragon who can't breathe fire? What am I going to do?

Narrator: The dragon spent a great deal of time feeling sorry for himself. Then one day, he had an idea.

Dragon: Since the witch put this spell on me, she must be able to take it off again! I'll ask her what I can do to get my fire back.

Narrator: And so the dragon stomped off through the forest until he came to the witch's cottage.

Dragon: Knock! Knock! Knock! Is anybody home?

Witch: You don't have to knock the door down! Oh, it's you, Dragon. What do you want? After I took your fire away, you said you never wanted to see me again.

Dragon: It's true. I did say that. But now I've come to do you a favor.

Witch: You have come to do ME a favor! Ha ha ha! What favor could a dragon who likes to burn brooms do for a witch?

Dragon: Well, even though I don't have my fire, I am still big and strong. Give me a difficult task. If I can do it, you can give me back my fire.

Witch: And if you can't?

Dragon: Then I promise never to bother you again.

Witch: Very well. It sounds like I can't lose! Let me think. Hmmmmm. . . . There is one little thing that I would like to have.

Dragon: Name it!

Witch: There was a little songbird that used to sing outside my window every morning and every evening. But she has flown away. If you can find that songbird and bring her back to me, then I'll lift the spell.

Dragon: I'm on my way!

Narrator: The dragon set off immediately in search of the songbird. After a time, he came to a tall tree beside a river. High up in the tree sat a bird that was singing a beautiful song.

Dragon: Hello, little songbird.

Bird: A dragon!

Dragon: Don't let me scare you. I'm really quite harmless. Tell me, have you lived here all your life?

Bird: No, Dragon. I used to live in a tree by the witch's cottage.

Dragon: Why did you leave?

Bird: I needed some straw to build my nest. But when the witch's broom got burned, she had no straw to give me. So I left in search of some.

Dragon: The witch misses your singing very much. If I find you some straw, will you go back and build your nest by the witch's cottage? If you do, the witch will give me back my fire.

Bird: Very well, if you find me some straw, I will build my nest by the witch's cottage, so the witch will give you back your fire.

Narrator: The dragon went off in search of some straw. At last he came to a farmer in a field.

Dragon: Good day to you, Farmer.

Farmer: A dragon!

Dragon: Don't let me scare you. I'm really quite harmless. And I've only come to ask you a very small favor.

Farmer: What is this small favor?

Dragon: Will you please cut me some straw, so the songbird can build her nest, so the witch will give me back my fire?

Farmer: Very well, but my horse needs new shoes before he can pull the mower. If you will shoe my horse, then I can cut the straw, so the songbird can build her nest, so the witch will give you back your fire.

Narrator: The dragon took the farmer's horse and went to find the blacksmith.

Dragon: Good day to you, Blacksmith.

Blacksmith: A dragon!

Dragon: Don't let me scare you. I'm really quite harmless. And I've only come to ask you a very small favor.

Blacksmith: What is this small favor?

Dragon: Will you please shoe the farmer's horse, so the farmer can cut his straw, so the songbird can build her nest, so the witch will give me back my fire?

Blacksmith: I would like to help you, Dragon. But as you can plainly see, my fire has gone out. Until the coals are hot again, I cannot shoe this or any other horse.

Dragon: If I can get your fire started, will you help me?

Blacksmith: Very well, if you can start my fire, I will shoe the farmer's horse, so the farmer can cut his straw, so the songbird can build her nest, so the witch will give you back your fire.

Dragon: I'll be back just as soon as I can.

Narrator: And with that, the dragon stomped off through the forest. Soon he was standing at the witch's door.

Dragon: KNOCK! KNOCK! KNOCK! It's me again.

Witch: Of course it's you. Nobody else knocks the door DOWN. Well, do you have my songbird?

Dragon: Almost.

Witch: ALMOST? Either you have the bird or you don't. And if you don't have the bird, you won't get your fire back.

Dragon: Dear Witch, I know where your songbird is, and I know how to bring her back.

Witch: Then what's the problem? Just bring her to me, and I'll return your fire.

Dragon: It's not as simple as that. You see, to bring her back to you, I must first have my fire.

Witch: What? Give you back your fire? Why, if I do that, you'll just disappear. Perhaps I should save us both a lot of trouble and make you disappear right now!

Dragon: Now don't be hasty, or we'll both be unhappy. You'll be unhappy because you won't have your songbird, and I'll be unhappy because I won't have . . . well, I won't have ME!

Witch: Very well, I guess I'll just have to trust you. Now, open wide, stick out your tongue, and say A-h-h-h-h-h!

Dragon: Will this hurt?

Witch: It will sting just a little. After all, you do want to breathe fire, don't you? Now hold still while I wave my magic wand. Fee, fie, foe, FIRE! There! The spell is broken!

Dragon: WHOOOOOSH! Ah, that's more like it. I'm a genuine dragon again. How can I ever thank you?

Witch: You can start by bringing me my songbird.

Dragon: Oh yes! In my excitement, I nearly forgot.

Narrator: The dragon stomped happily all the way to the blacksmith's shop, breathing fire in a friendly fashion at everyone he met.

Blacksmith: Well, I see you've come back. Do you have the fire?

Dragon: I certainly do! Please stand back!

Narrator: And the dragon breathed out a bright, hot flame. Soon the blacksmith's fire was roaring again . . .

Blacksmith: so I can shoe the farmer's horse,

Farmer: so I can cut my straw for the bird,

Bird: so I can build my nest in the tree by the witch's cottage,

Witch: so I can listen to my lovely songbird,

Dragon: so we (especially me) can all live

All: happily ever after!

A WHALE OF A STORY

by Judith Bauer Stamper

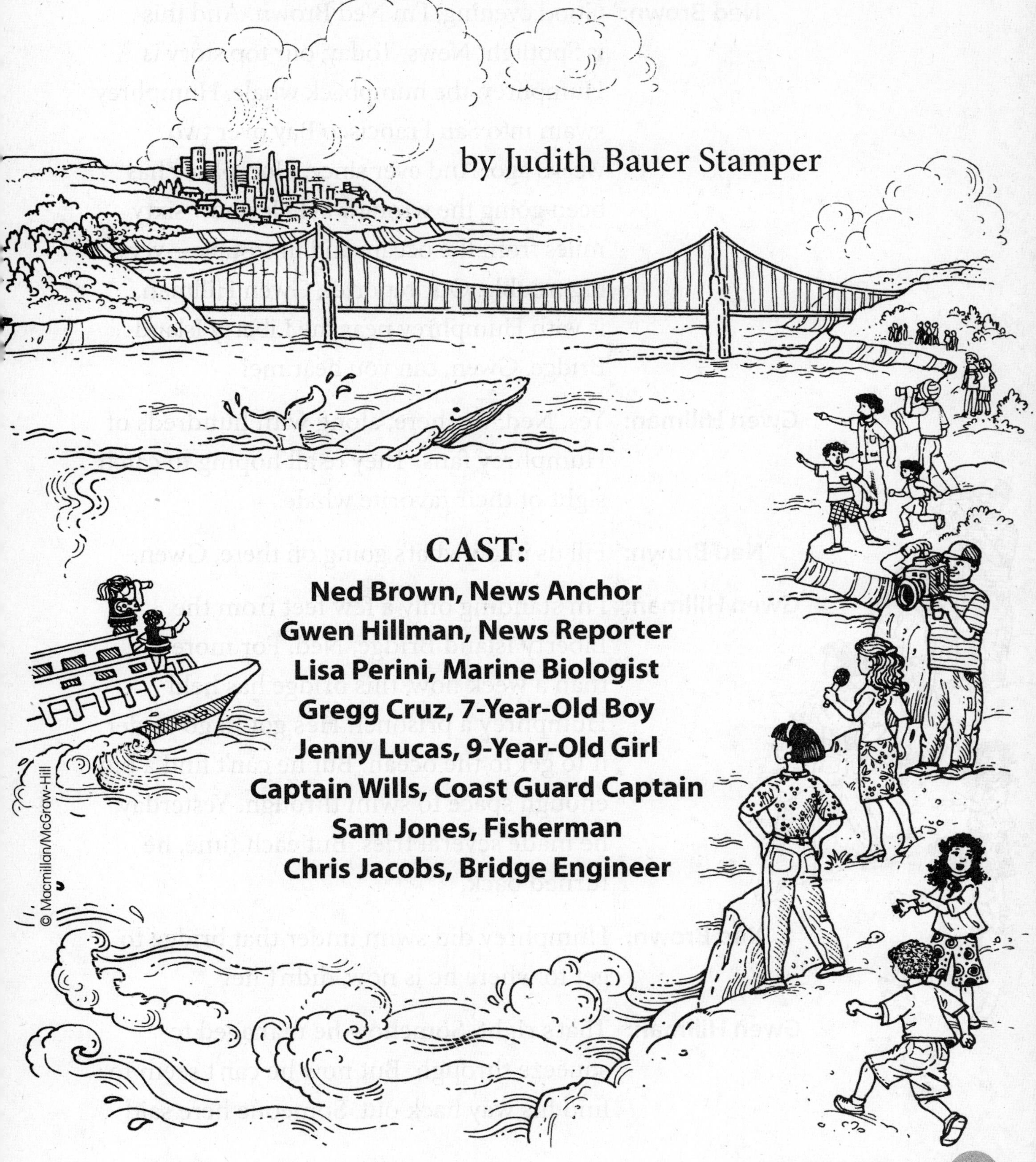

CAST:

Ned Brown, News Anchor
Gwen Hillman, News Reporter
Lisa Perini, Marine Biologist
Gregg Cruz, 7-Year-Old Boy
Jenny Lucas, 9-Year-Old Girl
Captain Wills, Coast Guard Captain
Sam Jones, Fisherman
Chris Jacobs, Bridge Engineer

Ned Brown: Good evening, I'm Ned Brown. And this is Spotlight News. Today, our top story is Humphrey, the humpback whale. Humphrey swam into San Francisco Bay over two weeks ago. And ever since, Humphrey has been going the wrong way! He's now sixty miles from the ocean, and in trouble—very big trouble. Our reporter, Gwen Hillman, is with Humphrey near the Liberty Island Bridge. Gwen, can you hear me?

Gwen Hillman: Yes, Ned. I'm here, along with hundreds of Humphrey fans. They're all hoping to catch sight of their favorite whale.

Ned Brown: Fill us in on what's going on there, Gwen.

Gwen Hillman: I'm standing only a few feet from the Liberty Island Bridge, Ned. For more than a week now, this bridge has held Humphrey a prisoner. He's got to go under it to get to the ocean. But he can't find a big enough space to swim through. Yesterday, he made several tries. But each time, he turned back.

Ned Brown: Humphrey did swim under that bridge to get to where he is now, didn't he?

Gwen Hillman: That's right. Somehow he managed to squeeze through. But now he can't seem to find his way back out. Someone here said

it's like being in a dark cave with a lot of passages. Think how hard it would be to find your way out.

Ned Brown: That sounds serious for Humphrey.

Gwen Hillman: It is, Ned. There're a lot of worried people here. They wonder how much longer Humphrey can survive. Let's talk to a few of them now. This is Lisa Perini, a scientist who's an expert on whales. Lisa, can you tell us how Humphrey is feeling?

Lisa Perini: Humphrey is in trouble, and I think he knows it. From watching him, I would say that this whale is stressed out.

Gwen Hillman: Just what do you mean by that, Lisa?

Lisa Perini: Look out over the water. I think he's going to do it again. Yes, there he goes, smacking his huge tail against the water.

Gwen Hillman: That made quite a splash! But what does it mean?

Lisa Perini: Humphrey is trying to signal other whales. He's smacking his tail to ask for help. That's what whales do in the ocean. But no other whales are around to hear or see him.

Gwen Hillman: Do you think Humphrey wants to get back to the ocean, Lisa?

Lisa Perini: Without a doubt, Gwen. Just think, Humphrey is a forty-ton whale. Right now he's trying to swim in water that's only ten feet deep in places! He must be scraping his belly on the bottom at times. And that has to hurt!

Gwen Hillman: Can a whale like Humphrey live in this water, Lisa? Isn't he used to ocean salt water?

Lisa Perini: Good point, Gwen. Whales belong in salt water. We're worried about what this fresh river water might do to Humphrey. It may be seeping through his skin. That could cause real problems. Before long, Humphrey could get waterlogged!

Gwen Hillman: What are Humphrey's chances of making it out of here alive, Lisa?

Lisa Perini: I think he can still make it, but this bridge is holding him back. Humphrey needs to get back to salt water—and soon!

Gwen Hillman: Thank you, Lisa. Back to you, Ned.

Ned Brown: What about all the children there, Gwen? How do they feel about Humphrey?

Gwen Hillman: Here's a boy right now wearing a Save -the-Whale T-shirt. Excuse me, could you answer a few questions? First tell us your name.

Gregg Cruz: I'm . . . um . . . Gregg Cruz. Am I really on television?

Gwen Hillman: Yes, you are, Gregg.

Gregg Cruz: Wow!

Gwen Hillman: Gregg, I see you are a fan of Humphrey's. What do you think will happen today?

Gregg Cruz: I hope he gets free! I come here every day on my bike to see him. It's almost like having a pet whale. But I know he's got to get back to the ocean. They have to find some way to help Humphrey.

Gwen Hillman: Thanks, Gregg. Here's another young person who looks interested in Humphrey. What's your name?

Jenny Lucas: I'm Jenny Lucas.

Gwen Hillman: Well, Jenny. What do you think of Humphrey?

Jenny Lucas: I think Humphrey is the most exciting thing I've ever seen. A real humpback whale in our own backyard! Humphrey has made me care about the whales more than I ever did before. You know, there are only about ten thousand humpback whales left in the whole world! So we just can't let this one die!

Gwen Hillman: Thanks, Jenny. You know, a lot of people are doing everything they can to save Humphrey. I see one of them right now, Coast Guard Captain Michael Wills. You are working to protect Humphrey, aren't you, Captain Wills?

Captain Wills: That's right, Gwen. Right now, the Coast Guard is doing its best to protect Humphrey from the boaters on the river.

Gwen Hillman: Did you say from the boaters, Captain? What do you mean?

Captain Wills: Lots of people wanted a close-up view of this whale. They were running their motorboats right up to him. Poor Humphrey was scared by the sound of their engines.

Gwen Hillman: What have you done to stop the boaters, Captain Wills?

Captain Wills: We've told them to clear out of the area. If necessary, we're ready to back up our words with action. That means up to a twenty-thousand-dollar fine!

Gwen Hillman: I'm sure the boaters are just curious. But they do have to think of Humphrey first. Ned, do you have any questions for Captain Wills?

Ned Brown: First of all, thank you for taking the time to speak with us today, Captain Wills.

Captain Wills: You're welcome, Ned. I'm a big fan of yours.

Ned Brown: Captain Wills, I'm hoping you can clear something up. We've been getting reports that the Coast Guard is banging on underwater pipes. Doesn't that scare Humphrey?

Captain Wills: As you know, Ned, whales are very sensitive to underwater sounds. Our hope is that Humphrey will swim away from the banging sounds toward the ocean.

Ned Brown: But where did you get the idea of banging on pipes?

Captain Wills: From Japanese fishermen, Ned. They bang on pipes to drive dolphins from their fishing nets. Yesterday, we tried doing the same thing with Humphrey.

Ned Brown: And how did it work, Captain Wills?

Captain Wills: Everything was going according to plan—until Humphrey reached the bridge. Then he stopped. Our feeling is that he's more frightened of the bridge than the pipes. We had to stop the banging because we didn't want to upset him.

Gwen Hillman: Thank you, Captain. Ned, as you may have seen on camera, Humphrey slapped his tail on the water again just seconds ago. There was a roar of excitement from this crowd. Here's someone right now who seems to want to say something. Hello, what's your name?

Sam Jones: I'm Sam Jones. I own a fishing boat. And I've been fishing around these parts for years.

Gwen Hillman: That's very interesting, Mr. Jones. And what would you like to share with our viewers?

Sam Jones: I'd just like to say that not enough has been done to save that whale.

Gwen Hillman: What do you suggest, Mr. Jones?

Sam Jones: I say we should lift him right out of the water with a helicopter. He wouldn't have to swim under the bridge. He could fly right over it!

Gwen Hillman: Really, Mr. Jones. Isn't that a little farfetched? How could you lift a whale by helicopter?

Sam Jones: Why, you could just put some straps around him and lift him right up.

Gwen Hillman: Well, Ned, that's just one of the ideas that people have come up with to save Humphrey. I wonder if Mr. Jones remembers that Humphrey weighs 40 tons and is 45 feet long. And I don't think he would let anybody put straps around him!

Lisa Perini: Excuse me, Gwen, but I just heard that man talking. That's not the only wild idea we've heard! Somebody else wanted to drop a trail of salt cubes in the river. Humphrey was supposed to follow them out to sea! That idea would never work. The salt would kill the plants and animals that live in the river.

Gwen Hillman: People care about Humphrey and want to help, but they just don't know what might work and what won't. Ned, do you have something you want to add?

Ned Brown: Just an interesting number. Over ten thousand people have called in with ideas about how to save Humphrey. But they've got to let the experts do the work.

Gwen Hillman: I have one of those experts here with me right now. This is Chris Jacobs. He's the engineer who has been working to help Humphrey get under the bridge. Hello, Chris.

Chris Jacobs: Hello, Gwen. I'm glad you're here with your crew because something exciting is going to happen any minute.

Gwen Hillman: What do you mean, Chris?

Chris Jacobs: We've been working on this bridge since yesterday. In fact, we worked all through the night, cleaning out the old wood and garbage on the river bottom. It was blocking the space between the wood pilings that hold up the bridge. Underwater, those pilings must have looked like shark's teeth to poor Humphrey! I'm hoping that today he'll make it through.

Gwen Hillman: I can see the boats out there right now. It looks as if they're trying to drive Humphrey toward the bridge. I can hear them banging on the underwater pipes again.

Jenny Lucas: Look! There's Humphrey! He's swimming in the direction of the bridge.

Gregg Cruz: Come on, Humphrey. You can do it!

Sam Jones: Go, Humphrey, go! Don't let that bridge stop you. You've got to get back to the ocean!

Gwen Hillman: Ned, the excitement is building up. People are standing on both sides of the river.

They're watching Humphrey make another try to get under the bridge. Will he make it? Lisa, what do you think his chances are?

Lisa Perini: I don't know, Gwen. But, look! Humphrey is getting closer and closer to the bridge. I just saw his back come out of the water. He's diving! He's trying to dive under the bridge!

Chris Jacobs: Oh no, he's stuck! I can see one of his fins. It's caught between two of the wood pilings.

Jenny Lucas: Can't somebody do something! What's going to happen to Humphrey?

Gwen Hillman: Ned, the crowd is holding its breath. This is a very dangerous moment for Humphrey. Lisa, what do you think the whale will do?

Lisa Perini: He's going to do everything he can to free himself. But I don't know if he'll be able to. Wait! Humphrey seems to be sinking! I can't see him anymore. He's sinking to the bottom of the river.

Gwen Hillman: Ned, the suspense is unbelievable. No one knows what's happened to Humphrey. Is he hurt? Is he resting? Wait, I see him coming out of the water! He's lifting one fin into the air. And he's squeezing through those two pilings.

Gregg Cruz: Go, Humphrey, go!

Jenny Lucas: You can do it, Humphrey!

Sam Jones : That's the way, Humphrey!

Gwen Hillman: He's done it! Humphrey's made it through the bridge! You can hear the people around here cheering. They are wild with excitement!

Chris Jacobs: He's going to be all right! I can see him on the other side of the bridge. And he's finally headed in the right direction—back to the ocean.

Gwen Hillman: What do you think, Lisa? Is Humphrey on his way home at last? Will he have enough strength to make it to the Pacific Ocean?

Lisa Perini: Gwen, I just got a good look at him when he came up out of the water. His skin seems to be in good shape. Humphrey also showed a lot of strength getting through those bridge pilings. I think he'll be all right.

Gwen Hillman: Captain Wills, I know you're going to have to get back to your boat soon. What is your next step in saving Humphrey?

Captain Wills: We'll try to keep Humphrey headed down the river. Instead of banging on the pipes, we'll start to use some tapes of the sounds whales make when they're feeding.

Lisa Perini: Let's just hope that Humphrey is hungry enough to follow these sounds right out to the ocean!

Gwen Hillman: Did you hear that roar of laughter, Ned? Humphrey just blew a fountain of water into the air. I think he's on his way home.

Ned Brown: This has been a great moment in a whale of a story. Thank you, Gwen. We'll be back later for an update on Humphrey as he makes his way back to the ocean. For now, that's all from Spotlight News.

THE SEARCH FOR THE MAGIC LAKE

based on an Ecuadorian folktale

by Merrily P. Hansen

CAST:

Emperor	**Farmer's Wife**
Voice of the Fire	**Farmer**
Empress	**First Sparrow**
Sumac	**Second Sparrow**
Magician	**Crab**
Prince	**Serpent**
First Son	**Alligator**
Second Son	**Guard**

Narrator: Long ago, the Incas were ruled by an emperor and an empress. They had a son who brought his parents great joy in all ways but one. He had been ill since birth. Not even the best doctors in the land could cure him.

Emperor: Each day our son grows weaker and weaker. None of the doctors know what to do. I fear he will die.

Empress: Husband, let us call on the gods in heaven. Perhaps they can tell us how to cure our son. We must go to the fire of the gods and beg for wisdom.

Narrator: A short time later, the emperor and empress bowed before the fire. They asked the gods for help.

Emperor: O Great Ones, I grow older. Soon I will join you in heaven. Who will look after my people if the prince is not well?

Empress: Please make our son well and strong. Tell us how he can be cured.

Voice of the Fire: O mighty rulers, there is only one cure for your son's illness.

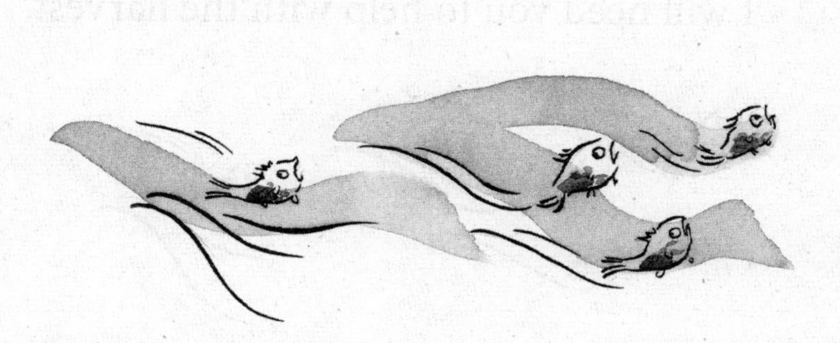

Emperor: Tell us! We will do anything.

Voice of the Fire: The prince must drink water from the magic lake at the end of the world. Then he will be cured.

Narrator: The fire died and grew cold. But among the ashes lay a golden flask.

Empress: The magic lake at the end of the world? I have never heard of such a place.

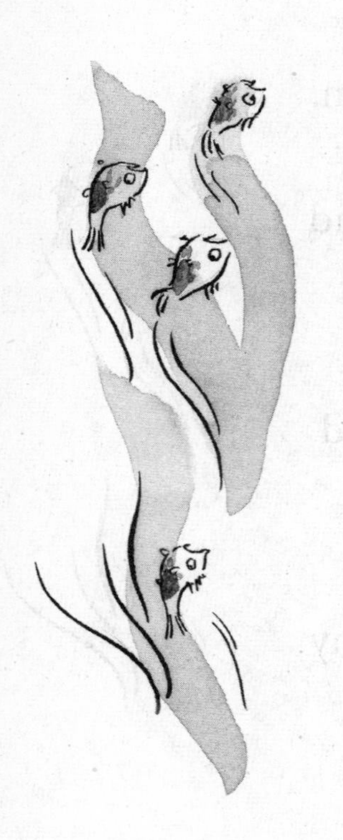

Emperor: The Voice of the Fire always speaks the truth. We must find the lake so that our son may be cured.

Narrator: The emperor was too old to make the long journey himself. So he had his messengers announce that anyone who could fill the golden flask with magic water would receive a great reward. Many brave people set out to find the lake. Weeks passed, and the flask remained empty. One day, news of the prince's illness reached a poor farmer and his family.

First Son: Father, my brother and I would like to search for the magic lake.

Farmer: It is too dangerous, my sons! Besides, I will need you to help with the harvest.

Second Son: We shall return before the moon is new again, to help with the harvest. We promise.

First Son: Just think of the rich reward, Father!

Farmer's Wife: Husband, it is their duty to go. We must all try to help the young prince.

Farmer: Go if you must. But beware of the wild animals in the hills.

First Son: We will be very careful, Father. Do not worry.

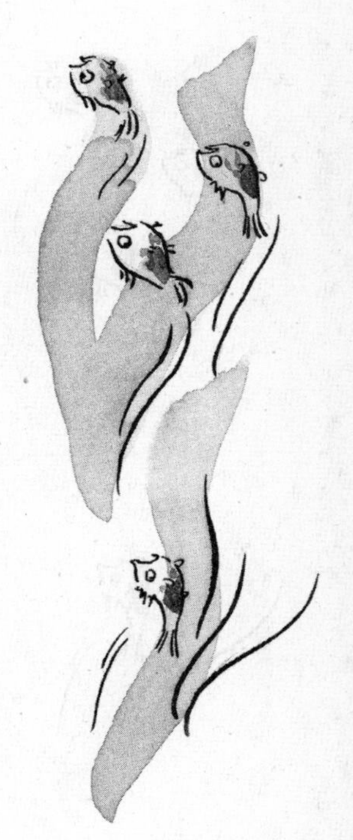

Narrator: The two brothers set out. They found many lakes, but none where the sky touched the water at the end of the world. Many weeks went by.

Second Son: Brother, it is time for us to return home. We promised to help father with the harvest.

First Son: You are right, but don't worry. I have a plan. Let us each fill a jar with water from the next lake we pass. We'll tell the emperor that the water is from the magic lake at the end of the world. Even if it does not cure the prince, we will surely receive a small reward for all our trouble.

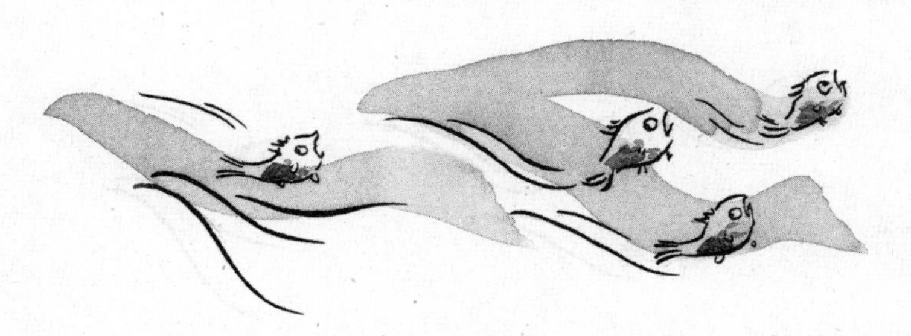

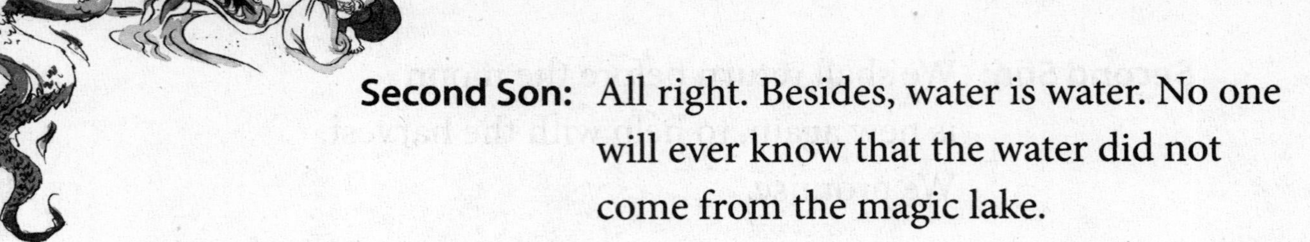

Second Son: All right. Besides, water is water. No one will ever know that the water did not come from the magic lake.

Narrator: When the brothers arrived at the palace, they gave the emperor the jars filled with water. Both of them said that the water had come from the magic lake.

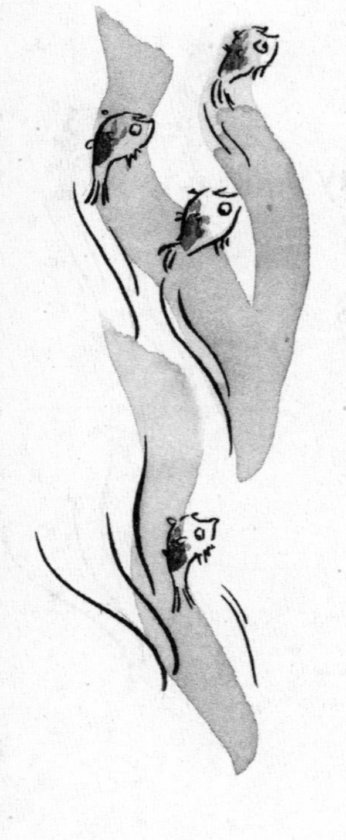

Emperor: Then one sip of water should cure the prince.

Empress: Hurry! Let us give him a taste of it.

Narrator: The prince took a sip from each jar of water.

Prince: Father, I don't feel any better.

Emperor: I have my doubts about this water!

First Son: Your majesty, perhaps the prince should drink it from the golden flask.

Second Son: That will probably make all the difference in the world!

Narrator: The emperor carefully poured a little water from each jar into the golden flask.

Emperor: My goodness! Look what is happening!

Empress: Why, the water is disappearing as you pour it! The flask is still empty.

First Son: That flask must be magic!

Second Son: Perhaps your magician could break the spell.

Narrator: The emperor called his magician to his side. He told him all that had happened.

Magician: Your majesty, I cannot break the spell of the golden flask.

Emperor: But you are my best magician! Of course you can break the spell.

Magician: No, your majesty, I cannot. I believe that the flask is telling us that we have been tricked. This is ordinary water! The golden flask can only be filled with water from the magic lake at the end of the world.

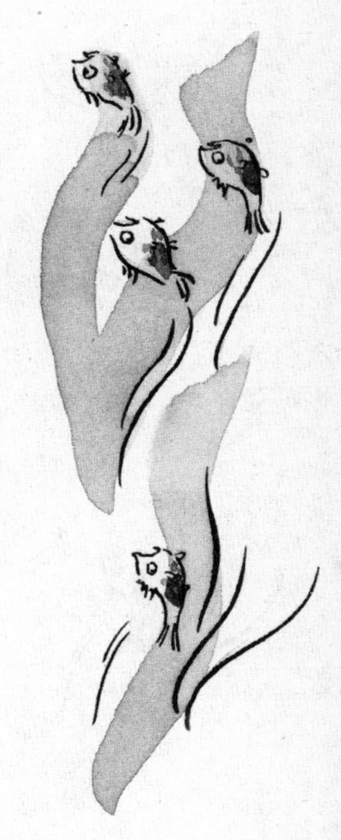

Emperor: So, you two have dared lie to me! You will spend the rest of your lives in chains. Each day you will drink water from your jars to remind you of your trickery.

Narrator: The two brothers were put in chains. Then once again, the emperor sent out his messengers. They told of the wicked brothers and the need to search again for the magic lake. Finally, the news reached Sumac, sister of the two brothers. She was tending her flock of llamas on a hill.

Sumac: I must tell Mother and Father the sad news about my brothers. Perhaps they will let me go in search of the magic lake.

Narrator: Sumac told her parents all she had heard.

Farmer: How could my sons do such a thing? I do not understand it.

Sumac: Father, they were wrong to do what they did. Now I must go to search in their place.

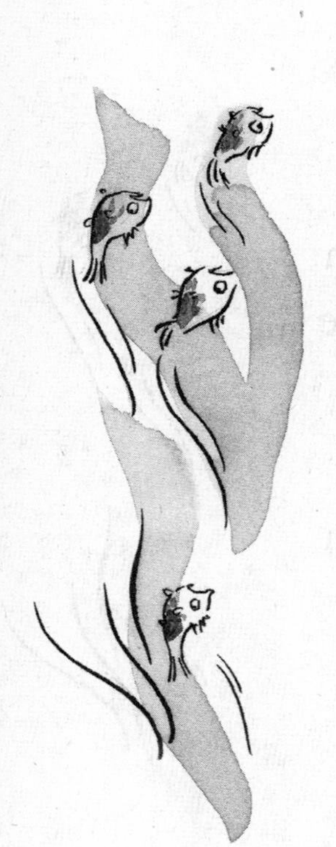

Farmer: No, no! A thousand times, no! You are too young. Besides, look what happened to your brothers.

Farmer's Wife: It is bad enough to have two children gone. What would we do if anything happened to you?

Sumac: But Mother, perhaps I can find the magic lake and save the prince. Then the emperor may forgive my brothers and send them home again.

Farmer's Wife: Dear husband, we should let Sumac go.

Farmer: Yes, you are probably right. She may be able to bring our sons home. And we must think of our emperor and his family, too.

Farmer's Wife: Go get one of the llamas. It can carry your blanket and keep you company. I will prepare food for your journey.

Narrator: When the llama was loaded, the family said goodbye. Sumac set out, leading the llama along the trail. The first night, she heard the cry of the wild puma. She feared for her llama, so the next morning she sent it home. The second night, Sumac slept in a tall tree. At sunrise she was awakened by the voices of some sparrows.

First Sparrow: Poor child. She will never be able to find her way to the magic lake.

Second Sparrow: Let us help her!

Sumac: Oh, please do! I beg your pardon, but I could not help overhearing. I hope you will forgive me for spending the night in your tree.

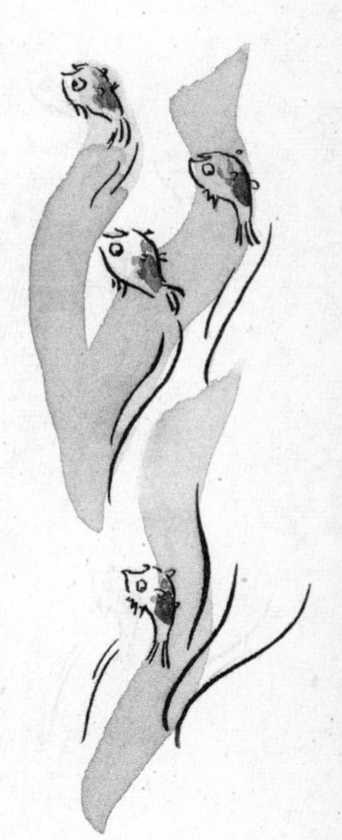

Second Sparrow: You are the girl who shared her food with us yesterday. You are quite welcome in our tree.

First Sparrow: We shall help you, because you are kind and generous. Each sparrow in our flock will give you a wing feather. Hold the feathers together to make a fan.

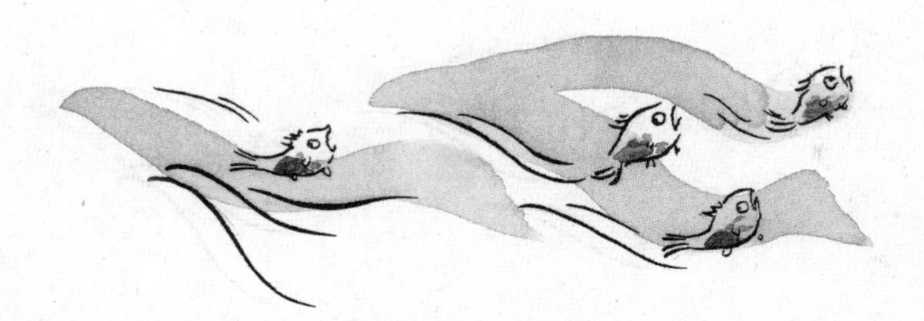

Second Sparrow: The fan has magic powers that will carry you wherever you wish to go. It will also keep you safe from harm.

Narrator: Each sparrow then lifted a wing and pulled a special feather hidden underneath. They gave the feathers to Sumac, who used a ribbon to fasten them into the shape of a little fan.

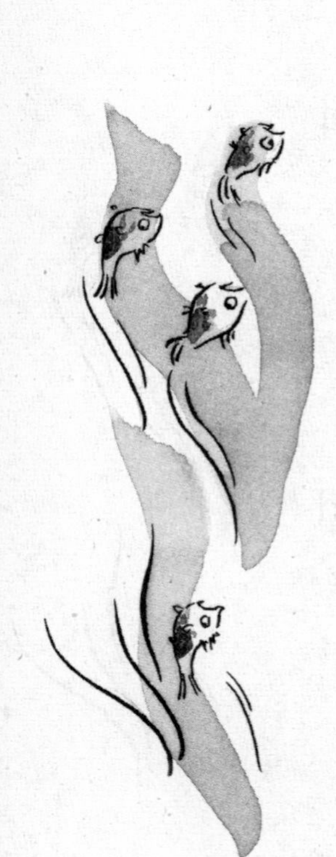

Second Sparrow: Listen well, little Sumac. I must warn you that the lake is guarded by three terrible monsters.

First Sparrow: But have no fear. If you hold the magic fan up to your face, you will be safe.

Narrator: Sumac thanked the birds for their kindness. Then she spread the fan and held it up.

Sumac: Please, magic fan. Take me to the lake at the end of the world.

Narrator: With that, a soft breeze began to blow. It picked up Sumac and carried her higher and higher into the sky. She looked down and saw the great mountains covered with snow. At last the wind put her down on the shores of a beautiful lake. Sumac looked across the lake to where the sky touched the water.

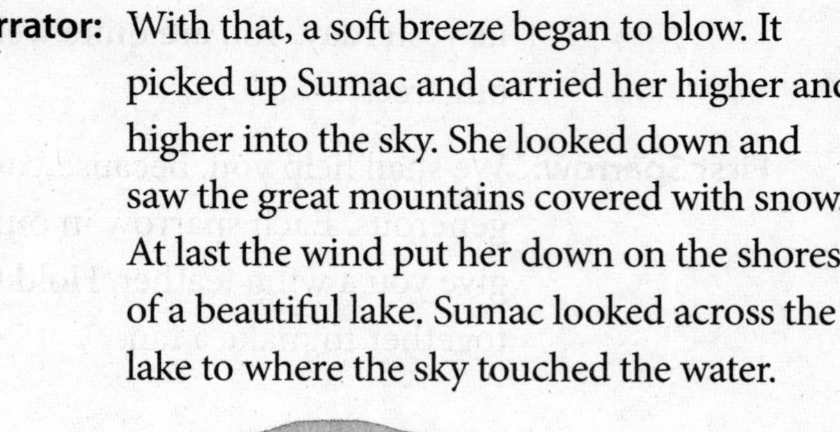

Sumac: This must be the lake at the end of the world!

Narrator: Sumac carefully tucked the magic fan into her belt. As she did so, she realized that she had forgotten something.

Sumac: Oh no! I left the jar back in the forest. How will I carry the water back to the prince?

Narrator: There was a soft thud at her feet. She looked down and discovered a beautiful golden flask. It was the same one that the emperor had found in the ashes of the fire of the gods. Sumac picked up the flask and went down to the lake. As she bent over, she heard a terrible hissing sound.

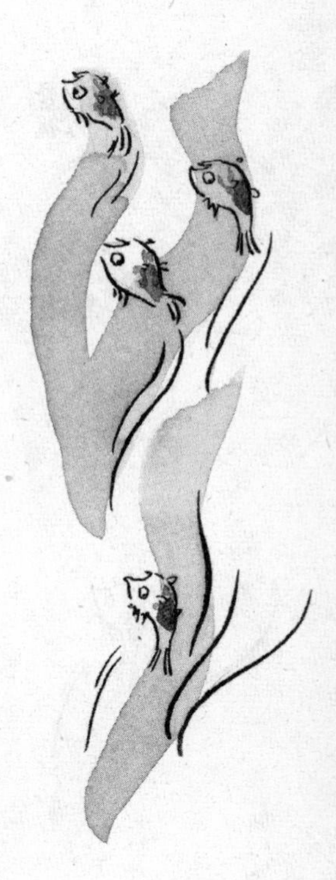

Crab: Just a moment. What do you think you are doing?

Narrator: Sumac turned and saw a giant crab. It was as large as a pig and as dark as the night.

Crab: Get away from my lake, or I shall wrap my long, hairy arms around you and carry you to the bottom!

Sumac: The sparrows said that the magic fan would protect me. I must trust in their promise.

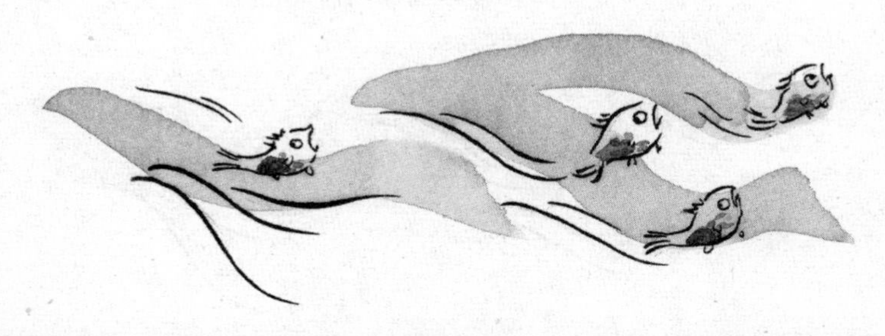

Narrator: Sumac spread the magic fan in front of her face. At once, the crab's eyes began to close.

Crab: What is happening? I feel so tired . . . I cannot keep my eyes open. Z-Z-Z-Z-Z-Z

Narrator: With that, the monster fell to the sand in a deep sleep. Quickly, Sumac began to fill the flask. This time she heard a strange bubbling noise. It was coming from a huge green log floating near the shore. Then the log began to speak.

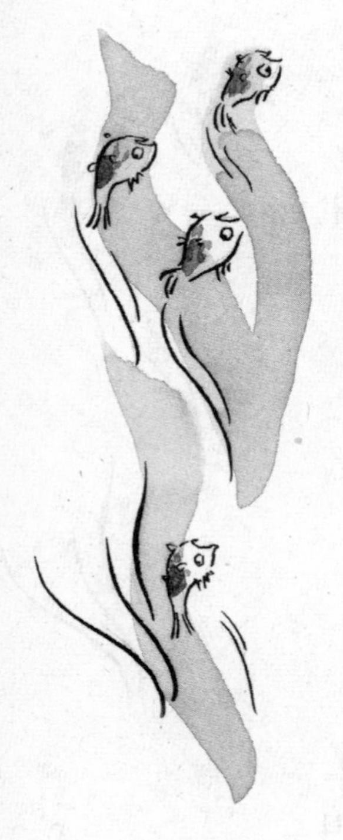

Alligator: Stop! You may not take water from this lake.

Sumac: It's another monster! That log is really a giant alligator!

Alligator: Get away from my lake, or I shall eat you!

Sumac: I must trust the fan once more.

Narrator: Sumac waited until the alligator swam closer. Then she opened the fan and held it up.

Alligator: What is happening? I feel so tired . . . I cannot keep my eyes open. Z-Z-Z-Z-Z-Z

Narrator: With that, the alligator slowly sank to the bottom of the lake in a sound sleep. A third time, Sumac began to fill the flask. All at once, she heard a shrill whistle.

Serpent: What are you doing? Who gave you leave to take water from the magic lake?

Narrator: Sumac looked up. There was a flying serpent. Its scales were as red as fire. Shining sparks flew from its eyes.

Serpent: Get away from my lake, or I shall bite you!

Sumac: I must hope that my magic fan will save me yet again.

Narrator: Sumac spread the fan and held it over her head near the serpent's open jaws.

Serpent: What is happening? I feel so tired . . . I cannot keep my eyes open. Z-Z-Z-Z-Z-Z

Narrator: The serpent closed its eyes and drifted slowly to the ground. Then the monster folded its wings and curled up in sleep. Sumac picked up the flask. This time she was able to fill it with water from the magic lake.

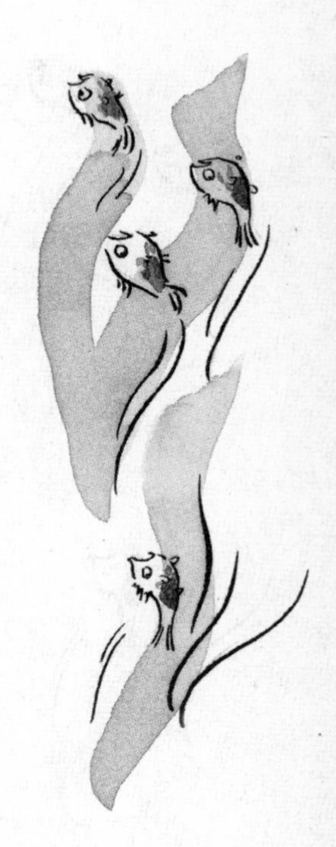

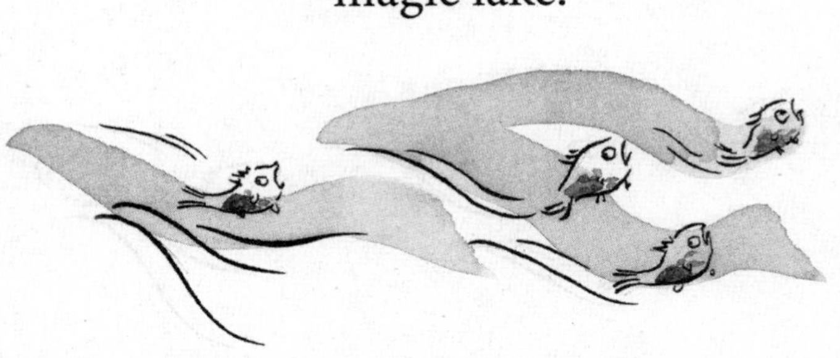

Sumac: Magic fan, please take me to the palace.

Narrator: As Sumac spoke these words, she found herself standing beside the palace gates looking up at a tall guard.

Sumac: Please, sir, I wish to see the emperor.

Guard: What business do you have with the emperor, little girl?

Sumac: I am Sumac. I bring water from the magic lake to cure the prince.

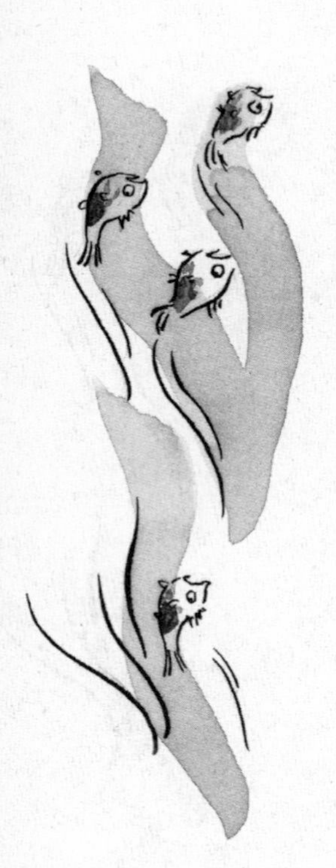

Guard: Come this way. I'll take you to see the emperor immediately!

Narrator: Sumac followed the guard through the palace. Finally, they came to a room with a huge bed. There lay the prince. The emperor and the empress stood by his side.

Guard: Your majesty, this is Sumac. She brings water from the magic lake!

Narrator: Sumac rushed to the bed to give the prince a few drops of the water.

Sumac: Dear prince! Taste this water. It is from the magic lake at the end of the world.

Empress: Look, his eyes are opening! See, his cheeks are becoming rosy!

Prince: How strong I feel! This must indeed be water from the magic lake.

Emperor: Dear child, you have saved my son's life! All the riches of my kingdom are not enough to reward you. Ask whatever you wish.

Sumac: Kind emperor, I have but three wishes.

Emperor: Name them, and they will be granted.

Sumac: First, I wish my brothers to be free. They have learned a hard lesson and will never lie again.

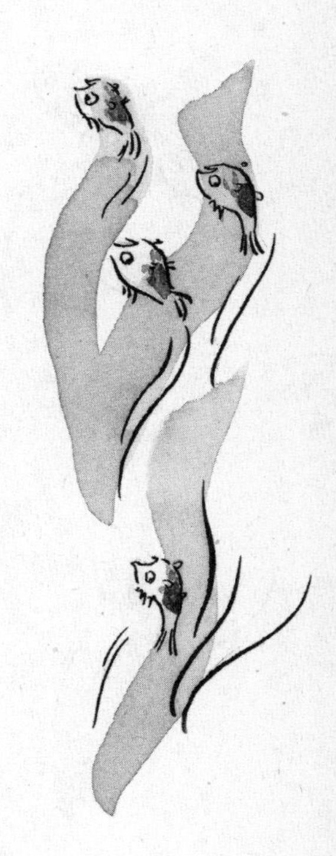

Emperor: Guards, free the two brothers at once! What is your second wish, my dear?

Sumac: I wish to have the magic fan returned to the sparrows in the forest.

Narrator: Before the emperor could speak, the magic fan floated out through the window, over the trees, and back to the forest.

Empress: What is your last wish, dear Sumac?

Sumac: I wish my parents to have a large farm with great flocks of llamas, so they will never be poor again.

Emperor: It will be so. But I am sure your parents never felt poor with such a wonderful daughter as you.

Prince: Sumac, won't you stay with us in the palace?

Empress: Yes, stay with us. We shall do all that we can to make you happy.

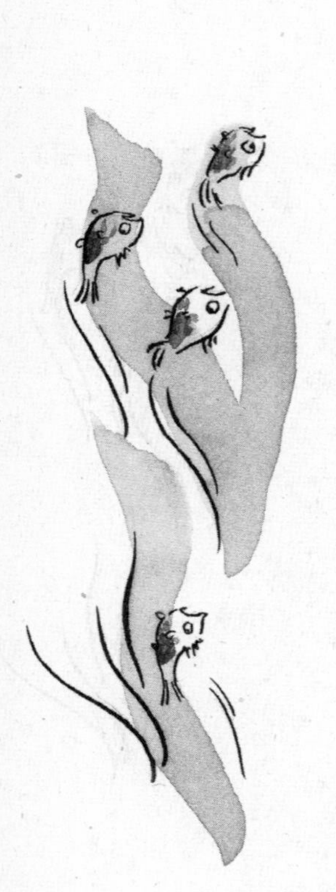

Sumac: Thank you for your kindness. But I must return to my family. I miss them, as I know they have missed me.

Narrator: When Sumac returned home, her family was waiting. Her parents now owned a rich farm. A beautiful new house and barn were soon built. And at the palace, the golden flask was never empty. The royal family lived long and happy lives.

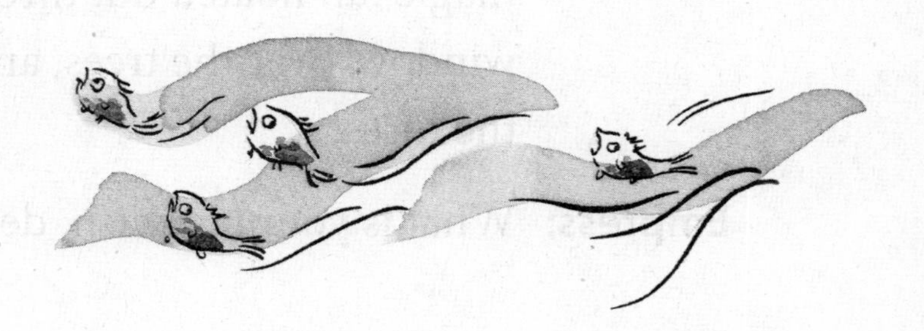

Mother Goose to the Rescue

by Joe Claro

CAST:

Mother Goose	**Cow**
Humpty Dumpty	**Willie Winkie**
King Cole	**Tommy Tucker**
Jack Horner	**Miss Muffet**

Humpty: This is the land of nursery rhymes. We'll happily sing you a song. We're usually cheerful. And not at all tearful, But once in a while things go wrong!

Mother Goose: Then I sit down with my paper and pen. No problem's too big or too small. When someone's upset, They write the Gazette. I have good advice for them all!

Humpty: Morning, Mother Goose. Here's your mail.

Mother Goose: Good morning, Humpty Dumpty. Oh, I do love getting all this mail! I'm so glad I switched from the Giving-Out-Jobs Department to the Giving-Out-Advice Department. Well, let's get to work. What do we have today?

Humpty: Here's a letter right on top from someone named Cole.

Mother Goose: Cole? Cole? Oh, yes, I remember. I found him a job as a king. Do we have a copy of that poem I wrote for him? It's been a while.

Humpty: Here it is, Mother Goose.

Old King Cole
Was a merry old soul,
And a merry old soul was he;
He called for his pipe,
And he called for his bowl,
And he called for his fiddlers three.

Mother Goose: Thank you, Humpty. What does King Cole say in his letter?

King Cole: Dear Mother Goose,

I have a problem, and I hope you can help. This morning I was sitting on my throne being merry, as usual. I decided to call for

my pipe, and a page brought it to me. Then I called for my bowl. Another page brought me one filled to the top with sweet red cherries.

Mother Goose: That sounds nice. Old King Cole certainly has a pleasant life. What kind of problem could he have?

King Cole: Everything was going just fine. Then I called for my fiddlers three. Fiddler One came in and played a snappy tune. Next, Fiddler Two came in and played a lovely waltz. Then Fiddler Three arrived. And that's when my problem began.

Mother Goose: Oh, good! A problem! Now he's going to ask me for advice.

King Cole: It was time for my nap, so Fiddler Three started to play "Rock-a-bye Baby." Screech! Screech! Screech! His fiddle sounded as squeaky as my old suit of armor! No one could sleep through that racket. What am I to do? I need my afternoon nap!

Sleepily,
King Cole

Mother Goose: Oh, how sad! Poor King Cole. Humpty, I'll dictate a letter and you write it. We'll print it in the afternoon edition of the Gazette.

Humpty: Go ahead. I'm ready.

Mother Goose: Dear King Cole,

I'm sorry to hear about your troubles. However, there's a simple answer. All you have to do is get a pair of earmuffs. Put them on and let Fiddler Three screech away. You won't hear a thing. Try it. You'll be asleep in no time at all.

Helpfully yours,
Mother Goose

Humpty: Excuse me, Mother Goose. Do you really think this is good advice?

Mother Goose: Of course it is! King Cole will be very grateful. Now, who sent the next letter?

Humpty: It's from one of the cows who used to work at the Rhymeland Dairy. Here's the poem you wrote for her:

Hey, diddle-diddle,
The cat and the fiddle,
The cow jumped over the moon;
The little dog laughed
To see such sport,
And the dish ran away with the spoon.

Mother Goose: My, my. That cow is one of the most talented athletes in Rhymeland. Let's hear her letter.

Cow: Dear Mother Goose,

Well, I did what you said in the rhyme you wrote for me. Now here I am, orbiting the earth. I don't like it up here. I'm the only cow in the neighborhood. How can I get back down to the dairy, where I belong?

Going around in circles,

The Cow

Mother Goose: Oh, my, that is a problem. Humpty, please take down this reply:

Dear Cow,

I must be honest with you. I never thought you'd be lonely in the Milky Way. But I do have a suggestion. As you orbit, watch for Rhymeland. When you see it, swish your tail back and forth as fast as you can. That should bring you back down to earth. See you soon.

Your friend,

Mother Goose

Humpty: Something tells me we won't be seeing her as soon as you think. This next letter is from Jack Horner. He lives behind the Rhymeland Bakery, remember? Here's the rhyme you wrote for him.

Little Jack Horner
Sat in the corner,
Eating a Christmas pie;
He put in his thumb,
And pulled out a plum,
And said, "What a good boy am I!"

Mother Goose: And he is a very good boy indeed. What's troubling him?

Jack Horner: Dear Mother Goose:

I've been doing the job you assigned me every day for six months. I now have plums everywhere! I've got plums in the kitchen, plums in the basement, and plums in my closet. My garage is filled with plums. Please tell me what to do! Fast!

Worriedly,
Jack Horner

Mother Goose: That boy does need my advice! Humpty, please write down this answer:

Dear Jack,

From now on, after you've pulled out a plum, simply eat it. As for your present problem, there's only one solution. Move immediately!

Your friend,
Mother Goose

P.S. I hear Mother Hubbard has a bare cupboard. You could take some plums over to her place.

Humpty: This next letter is from that boy with the night job. Here's his rhyme. Wee Willie Winkie runs through the town, Upstairs and downstairs, in his nightgown. Rapping at the window, crying through the lock, "Are the children in their beds? Now it's eight o'clock."

Willie: Dear Mother Goose,

I'm writing because I need your advice. You see, I sleep during the day and I work at night. I go around to make sure all the children in Rhymeland are in bed by eight o'clock.

Mother Goose: I'm sure their parents like that. What could be wrong?

Willie: Now, here's my problem. I set my alarm clock for seven o'clock at night. That gives me just enough time to get up and brush my teeth before I go out and rap on windows and rattle locks. But my alarm clock just broke, and I'm afraid I'll oversleep. What should I do?

Alarmingly yours,
Wee Willie Winkie

Mother Goose: Poor little lad. He has a perfect on-time record. No wonder he's worried. Humpty, please take this down:

Dear Willie,

Your problem is a simple one. And it has a simple solution. Get a rooster. Put him on your night table. Ask the rooster to stand on his head. By doing this, he will do everything backwards. Instead of crowing at seven o'clock in the morning, he'll crow at seven o'clock at night. See? I told you it was simple.

Helpfully yours,
Mother Goose

Humpty: Now we move on to a letter from Little Tommy Tucker. Remember him? He's the boy with the golden voice.

Little Tommy Tucker
Sings for his supper:
What shall we give him?
White bread and butter.

Mother Goose: Of course I remember Tommy. He's hoping to make TV commercials. What does he have to say?

Tommy: Dear Mother Goose,

It's been a great year. I've been singing for my supper every night. And every night I get that white bread and butter that I love so much. Now here's my problem. I woke up this morning with a sore throat. The doctor told me not to sing until it gets better. What should I do?

Musically yours,
Little Tommy Tucker

Mother Goose: Humpty, please take this down:

Dear Tommy,

Gargle.

Healthfully yours,
Mother Goose

P.S. You really should try to cut down on the butter. All that fat isn't good for you.

Humpty: Maybe he ought to try some soup. Here's the last letter, Mother Goose. It's from Little Miss Muffet.

Little Miss Muffet
Sat on a tuffet,
Eating her curds and whey;
There came a big spider,
Who sat down beside her
And frightened Miss Muffet away.

Mother Goose: Poor thing. I can't believe I made up that job for such a sweet, young girl! What does Miss Muffet have to say?

Miss Muffet: Dear Mother Goose,

You'll be happy to know that because of this job, I'm doing very well in my science class. I know more about spiders than anyone else at school.

Mother Goose: Oh, I was so right to give her that job!

Miss Muffet: But I have a problem. Actually, I have two problems. The first is with my curds and whey. I know they both come from milk. But I can't remember which is which. I'm afraid I may be eating my whey and curds, instead of my curds and whey.

Mother Goose: Oh, my. And what's her second problem?

Miss Muffet: My second problem is that tuffet. Could you please tell me what a tuffet is? I can't sit on one unless I know what it is!

Curiously,
Little Miss Muffet

Humpty: I've often wondered what a tuffet is. And I don't know what curds and whey are, either. What reply do you want me to print, Mother Goose?

Mother Goose: Reply? What do you mean?

Humpty: Why, a reply to Little Miss Muffet's letter. Aren't you going to answer her questions?

Mother Goose: H-m-m-m. I don't think so.

Humpty: Why, Mother Goose! You don't know the answers, do you? You wrote the poem, but you don't know what a tuffet is.

Mother Goose: Well, I do know that tuffet rhymes with Muffet. And that's what counts when you're writing nursery rhymes!

Humpty: And how about curds and whey?

Mother Goose: I did know the difference once. But that was a long time ago.

Humpty: So, what should we tell Little Miss Muffet?

Mother Goose: I don't know. Wait! I've got it! We'll solve her problems by giving her a new job.

Humpty: What do you mean?

Mother Goose: Miss Muffet's first name is Mary, isn't it?

Humpty: Why, yes. I think it is.

Mother Goose: Wonderful! Miss Muffet said she's doing well in her science class. That means she must like school. Well, I've been working on a rhyme about a lamb that follows a girl named Mary to school. Let's bring Miss Muffet into the office and talk to her about this new job.

Humpty: Okay. I'll call her. Then I'll drop these letters off at the printer's shop.

Mother Goose: Thank you, Humpty.

Humpty: Right! See you later.

Mother Goose: Here in the land of nursery rhymes,
Things often go wrong, as you see. Got a problem or two? I know just what to do.
So relax, and leave it to me!

Think-Aloud COPYING MASTERS

I wonder . . .

I made a connection when . . .

I was able
to picture
in my mind . . .

I figured out
______ because . . .

I noticed the
author used . . .

I thought ______
was important in this
text because . . .

This was mostly
about . . .

When I read ______,
I had to re-read,
read back, read on . . .

LITERATURE INDEX by GENRE

Biography

Fiction

Folktales, Fairy Tales, and Fables

Nonfiction

Plays

Poetry

ACKNOWLEDGMENTS Continued

"Nail Soup" from DEBI GLIORI'S BEDTIME STORIES: BEDTIME TALES WITH A TWIST by Debi Gliori. Copyright © 2002 by Debi Gliori. Used by permission of DK Publishing, Inc.

THIS IS OUR EARTH by Laura Lee Benson. Copyright © 1994 by Charlesbridge Publishing. Used by permission of Charlesbridge Publishing.

CLOUDY WITH A CHANCE OF MEATBALLS by Judi Barrett. Copyright © 1978 by Judi Barrett. Used by permission of Aladdin Books, an imprint of Simon & Schuster Children's Publishing Division.

"Slowly Does It" by Robin Ravilious from ANIMAL STORIES FOR THE VERY YOUNG selected and edited by Sally Grindley. Copyright © 1994 by Robin Ravilious. Used by permission of Kingfisher, Larousse Kingfisher Chambers Inc.

Excerpt from THE DESERT IS THEIRS by Byrd Baylor. Copyright © 1975 by Byrd Baylor. Used by permission of Charles Scribner's Sons.

ALBERT'S PLAY by Leslie Tryon. Copyright © 1992 by Leslie Tryon. Used by permission of Atheneum, a division of Macmillan Publishing Company.

LEWIS AND CLARK: A PRAIRIE DOG FOR THE PRESIDENT by Shirley Raye Redmond. Copyright © 2003 by Shirley Raye Redmond. Used by permission of Random House Children's Books.

KATE AND THE BEANSTALK by Mary Pope Osborne. Copyright © 2000 by Mary Pope Osborne. Used by permission of Atheneum Books for Young Readers, an imprint of Simon & Schuster Children's Publishing Division.

"A Dress for the Moon" by Indira Krishnan from Highlights for Children, Dec. 2003, Vol. 58, Issue 12. Copyright © 2003 by Highlights for Children. Used by permission of Highlights for Children.

WHEN ELEPHANT GOES TO A PARTY by Sonia Levitin. Copyright © 2001 by Sonia Levitin. Used by permission of Rising Moon.

IF YOU WERE A WRITER by Joan Lowery Nixon. Copyright © 1988 by Joan Lowery Nixon. Used by permission of Aladdin Paperbacks, an imprint of Simon & Schuster Children's Publishing Division.

SO YOU WANT TO BE AN INVENTOR? by Judith St. George. Copyright © 2002 by Judith St. George. Used by permission of Philomel Books, a division of Penguin Putnam Books for Young Readers.

"The Search for the Magic Lake" is based on "The Search for the Magic Lake" from LATIN AMERICAN TALES by Genevieve Barlow. Copyright © 1966 by Rand McNally & Company. Used by permission of Genevieve Barlow.

"The Bremen Town Musicians" from THE OLD WOMAN AND HER PIG & TEN OTHER STORIES by Anne Rockwell. Copyright © 1979 by Anne Rockwell. Used by permission of Dystel & Goderich Literary Management.

THE GREAT KAPOK TREE: A Tree of the Amazon Rain Forest by Lynne Cherry. Copyright © 1990 by Lynne Cherry. Reprinted by permission of Houghton Mifflin Harcourt Publishing Company. All rights reserved.

Cover Illustration: Janet Montecalvo

Illustration Credits: Brian Langdo, 9–13; Stephen Marchesi, 14–16, 58–62; Nicole in den Bosch, 17–21; Gioia Fiammenghi, 28–33; Madeline Sorel, 34–37; Tatjana Mai-Wyss, 38–41 ; Carol Koeller, 42–45; Amanda Harvey, 46–50, 112–116; Betsy James, 51–53, 192–206; Susan Spellman, 54–57, 117–123; Ashley Mims, 63–67, 153–156; Kathleen Kemly, 68–72; Ka Botzis, 73–77; Kelly Murphy, 83–87; Renee Daily, 88–90; Margeaux Lucas, 91–96; Kate Flanagan, 97–101; Joel Snyder, 102–107; Paige Billin-Frye, 108–111; Valerie Sokolova, 124–127; Bridget Starr Taylor, 128–132; Janet Montecalvo, 133–139; Hector Borlasca, 140–144; Laurie Harden, 145–152; Yvette Banek, 158–164; Ruth Flanigan, 165; Neecy Twinem, 166–178; Eva Cockrille, 179–191; Terri Murphy, 207–218